The Franchising Handboo

D0247475

This, my second book, is dedicated to my family – my wife Sarah, who is an amazing support both at home and in my business, and my wonderful children: Jordan, Lauren, Daisy and Charlie, together with our new arrival who is expected in 2016.

I'd also like to dedicate this book to the franchising community both in the UK and internationally. As a close-knit group, we are all fighting to improve the recognition and standing of ethical business format franchising; and I hope that this book goes some way towards helping that mission.

The Franchising Handbook

How to choose, start and run a successful franchise

Carl Reader

First published in Great Britain in 2016 by Hodder and Stoughton. An Hachette UK company.

This edition published in 2016 by John Murray Learning

British Library Cataloguing in Publication Data: a catalogue record for this title is available from the British Library.

Library of Congress Catalog Card Number: on file.

Paperback ISBN 978 1 47362 111 4

eBook ISBN 978 1 47362 112 1

2

Typeset by Cenveo® Publisher Services.

Printed and bound in Great Britain by CPI Group (UK) Ltd., Croydon, CR0 4YY.

John Murray Learning policy is to use papers that are natural, renewable and recyclable products and made from wood grown in sustainable forests. The logging and manufacturing processes are expected to conform to the environmental regulations of the country of origin.

Carmelite House
50 Victoria Embankment
London EC4Y 0DZ
www.hodder.co.uk

Contents

About the Author

I've advised thousands of businesses over the past 15 or so years, on a range of matters from simple bookkeeping and administration through to selling and even potential flotation on stock markets. In particular, over the past ten years I have focused on franchising, and I hope that this book will distil some of my knowledge in that area and help you understand more about business format franchising as a concept. My sole aim with this book is to help you enter into franchising with your eyes open – to know what to look for, where to take advice, and how to choose, start and run a successful franchise.

My life in business started very early, in a very humble way. I can't lie and pretend that I was a child genius, but I guess the entrepreneurial spirit has always been with me. From an early age I grew up on a council estate in Shoeburyness, Essex, and as kids we would buy bottles of Happy Shopper lemonade to split into glasses, so that we could sell them to the other kids who weren't allowed to the shops on their own. Later on in life, at about 10 or 11, we were living in an area called Rayleigh, where together with some friends we would go around the neighbourhood washing cars to earn some money for magazines and sweets. I guess that with these experiences I learned a lot about finding a market, the benefits of a captive market, providing a product, pricing strategies (we had already cottoned on to different levels of washing, and differential pricing for differently sized cars!) and keeping customers happy.

I was never particularly academic, despite always doing reasonably well in exams and tests, and left school early to start a YTS (Youth Training Scheme) in hairdressing, returning only to complete my GCSE exams. After then applying for every job in the local paper, I had an interview at two accountancy practices and the Army – I must have worked in alphabetical order! I was clearly more suited to advisory work as I was offered both accountancy jobs, and from there I started looking after businesses of all shapes and sizes.

I'm now fortunate enough to be a joint owner of a large local practice, which has won both the Independent Firm of the Year (South West) in the British Accountancy Awards, and was also awarded Most Innovative Medium Sized Firm of the Year by the 2020 Group. It is truly the UK's market leader in its niche markets of children's tuition businesses and franchised businesses. In particular, we are now the accredited accountancy provider for more than 130 brands, including some very well known names. Through this I've also been featured personally in *Accountancy Age*'s '35 under 35', which is a showcase of young talent in the industry, and have been a finalist for the British Accountancy Awards Practitioner of the Year.

I've also been involved in other businesses, together with sitting on the board of two not-for-profit organizations, acting as a funding panel member for the Fredericks Foundation, and as a committee member for the British Franchise Association (bfa). Recently, I was delighted to have been re-elected as the Affiliate Forum Chair at the bfa by my professional adviser colleagues, and have been helping the social franchise The Trussell Trust with some pro bono consulting to help them develop their franchised network of food banks.

Please bear in mind that there are themes within this book that could form a book in their own right, and there are plenty of additional resources available should you wish to explore a particular area further. In particular, you might find that my first book, *The Startup Coach*, will provide you with more information about the nuts and bolts of starting a business (albeit aimed at general business rather than specifically at franchising).

Finally, it would be great to hear about your success stories after using this book! Please feel free to contact me using the following methods. I'd love to hear from you.

Twitter – www.twitter.com/CarlReader

Facebook – www.facebook.com/CarlReader

Website – www.carlreader.com

Acknowledgements

I would like to thank the following who have helped shape this book in some way, through their contributions, expert advice, quotes or case studies (in order of contribution): Euan Fraser, Hilary Coates, Michael Bohan, David Holland, Clive Smith, Matt Snell, Pip Wilkins, Dave Williams, Derrick Simpson, Jon Bellamy, Ken Deary, Fiona Corallini, Simon Bartholomew, Louise Harris, Simon Mills, Steve Felmingham, Anne-Marie Martin, Mike Parker, Dave Galvin, Rob Oyston, Laurence Bagley, Suzie McCafferty, Phil Harrison, Jo Tomlinson, Steven Frost, Kelly Chambers-Lee, Bev Regan, Nicola Broadhurst, John Pratt, Damian Humphrey, Nina Moran-Watson, Andrew Fraser, Chris Roberts, Mark Scott, Chris Cook, Jeff Longley, Brian Duckett, Lucy Maisey, Freddie St George, Cathryn Hayes, Gordon Drakes, Russell Ford, Graeme Payne, Julie Taylor, and Jane Masih, who provided the sample franchise agreement towards the end of the book. Without your help this book would have had far less of an impact – the words of those who've been there, seen it and done it are far better than the words from outside of your own expertise and experiences. Each contributor gave up his or her own time to provide some amazing content to help inform you, the reader.

I'd also like to offer a special thanks to Paul Stafford of the British Franchise Association for his help with various areas of the book, not least providing me with up-to-date statistics from the NatWest/bfa 2015 Franchise Survey on a bank holiday just before the publishing deadline.

I'd also like to thank my editors, Alison Pickering and Iain Campbell, who have performed an amazing job of translating my (sometimes hazy) words into the book that you are holding today. Thank you.

Praise for *The Franchising Handbook*

"Buying a franchise is a big decision so it's important to do everything you can to maximize your chances of success. *The Franchising Handbook* is a thoroughly comprehensive guide for prospective franchisees. Written in refreshingly plain English and laid out in a user-friendly format, it is packed full of helpful tips and recommendations from leading industry experts. It provides particular guidance with respect to selecting and evaluating franchise opportunities, including the all-important questions to ask a prospective franchisor and what to expect from the franchisor/franchisee partnership. It's essential reading for anyone thinking of buying a franchise for the first time."

Julia Choudhury, Corporate Development Director, Franchise Brands

"Carl has gleaned a wealth of experience in franchising from working with some of the UK's biggest franchise brands. This book shares with the reader that accumulated knowledge and is an essential resource for franchisor and franchisee alike."

Dan Archer, Franchise Professional

"Carl's enthusiasm and passion for business is second to none and his knowledge of the franchise sector comes from his ability to get in front of the right people. This potent mix forms the backbone of *The Franchising Handbook*, an informative and necessary read for anyone considering embarking on life as a franchisee."

Craig Brown, MD Signs Express (franchisor)

"Carl is highly respected by the franchise community and I've had the pleasure of attending his seminars. Within the pages of *The Franchising Handbook* he has distilled that self-same charisma and knowledge to bring his enthusiasm and expertise to a greater audience."

**Graham Duckworth, Franchise Sales Director,
Driver Hire Group Services Ltd**

"Carl is obviously an expert in his field and therefore the right person to put this work together; the franchising world needs a signposting publication like this."

Andrew Brattesani, UK Head of Franchising, HSBC

Author's note

You will see that throughout the text there are a number of contributions from various members of the UK franchising community. I have grouped the advisory contributions as follows:

Case study: these are real-life examples of what has been encountered by either a franchisor or a franchisee within their own businesses.

Advice/view from a franchisor: these sections, entitled **Remember this**, provide feedback from franchisors who have seen a range of franchisees in their business. I've deliberately chosen a range of franchisors – both in respect of the specific sectors that they currently trade in, but also in respect of their experience. The reason for this is that some mature franchisors are not actively recruiting for new territories, and in these cases the input from newer franchisors is potentially more relevant. I've also aimed to get a good mix between entrepreneurs who have franchised their own business, and employed franchise directors who have worked with a number of brands, since I believe that this variety can help you, the reader, gain as much insight about the wider franchising industry as possible.

Advice from an expert: nobody in franchising is an expert in every area. For this very reason I have asked some trusted colleagues to provide some input in relation to their specialist areas and these are to be found in sections entitled **Key idea**. While a number of these advisers act for franchisors, they have kindly agreed to impart their knowledge and expertise for you to help you decide whether franchising is right for you, and to help you choose the right franchise.

An important point to make is that no payment or benefit has been received by the author or the publisher from any of the contributors to this book. In an effort to ensure that the integrity of the advice and case studies is maintained, there are no 'advertorial' sections. All contributions have been selected based on my experience of working with or alongside the contributors in the UK franchising community, and are unedited viewpoints as far as possible.

Ensuring the integrity of the advice has also led to a potentially confusing area that needs to be addressed. You will note that in some areas there is reference to 'franchise owner' rather than 'franchisee'. Within the franchising world there is some dispute as to whether franchisees should or should not be referred to as franchise owners, given that ultimate ownership of the brand and operating systems lies with the franchisor, yet ownership of the locally generated business goodwill lies with the franchisee (hence, the opportunity for franchisees to sell on their business). While in the main text I have used the phrase 'franchisee' for simplicity and to avoid confusion, where an expert has used the phrase 'franchise owner' I have kept the advice intact to maintain the originally intended tone of the message.

You will note that some sections of the advisory pieces and case studies are in bold type for emphasis. The sections that are emphasized have been picked out to reinforce the key messages within the text.

Part One

Introduction

1

What is a franchise?

In this chapter you will learn:

▶ *The history of business format franchising, both in the UK and internationally*
▶ *The types of business that are franchised*
▶ *The key elements of a franchise*
▶ *Why a business might decide to franchise.*

First, thank you for picking up this book! There is a lot of confusion and mystique around franchising, and due to the way that franchising has developed over the years it's safe to say that there really are elements of 'the good, the bad and the ugly' in the franchise world. Having said that, once you are aware of what to look out for, purchasing a franchise can be a life-changing event for all the right reasons, and can set you on the path towards financial freedom.

Many people have heard of franchised brands, such as McDonald's and Subway; however, they might be surprised as to the sheer scale of franchising in both the UK and worldwide.

In the UK there are 901 active franchisors and 44,200 franchised outlets (NatWest/bfa 2015 Franchise Survey). The industry is responsible for employing 621,000 people, and makes a £15.1 billion contribution to the nation's gross domestic product (GDP).

On a worldwide basis, franchising is even more popular, with nations such as the US and Australia embracing franchising as a generally accepted part of their entrepreneurial culture. Even countries coming out of crisis are adopting franchising – for example, I've been involved in assisting a contingent of Tunisian professionals who are looking to build a professional approach to franchising following the Arab Spring.

In this book you will find various case studies and advice pieces from experienced franchisors and franchise experts. Some of these cover similar areas, and with good reason; some things are so important that they're worth hearing several times over.

Everyone who has contributed to this book is someone who I have some experience of working with, and in turn trust to provide ethical, honest and impartial advice. Their input is perhaps the most valuable thing that you can take from this book – consider their tips to be a collection of the best-possible advice that you can follow to ensure that you choose and run a successful franchise!

The history of franchising

The first signs of franchising can be traced back to feudal England, when lords allowed peasants certain rights on part of their land in return for a fee (to perform tasks such as operating wells for water provision or running a market, for example). Components of a franchise system could also be found in the provision of resources for an army by local lords and chiefs in return for tax-collecting privileges.

Many years later, franchising became more entrenched in the UK with the advent of the tied pub system. Following the introduction of legislation making it very expensive to keep and maintain a public house in the 18th century, licensees began to struggle to operate successfully. Recognizing that it was in their interests to have a secure and stable market for their products, brewers began to offer publicans the opportunity of financial support in return for exclusivity over what was sold in the pub. Thus a familiar system – that remains widely used in the licensed trade today – was born.

The origins of franchising as it's come to be known and defined today can be clearly pinpointed to one man: Isaac Singer. After the American Civil War in the 1860s, Singer had achieved the ability to mass-produce his famous sewing machines, but had no economically viable way of repairing and maintaining them across a country as geographically vast as the United States.

He began to license out servicing and repairs to local merchants around the country, who were later permitted to become regional salesmen for the machines too. Singer's use of a contract for this arrangement introduced the earliest form of franchise agreements, and the first modern franchise system was born.

Over the following century, forms of franchising became more widely used in the US as a way to standardize products and standards from one coast to another. First was the car dealership model pioneered by General Motors in the early 20th century, granting exclusive rights and territories; then oil companies and grocery stores began to take advantage of a business model that offered them a route of fast growth towards national distribution with reduced risk.

After the Second World War franchising grew rapidly, propelled by companies looking to expand quickly. Soft drinks giants like Coca-Cola and Pepsi couldn't operate economically US-wide with such a high water content in their products and expensive transportation relative to its cost, so they developed a franchise system whereby franchisees would carbonate and add water to the companies' centrally manufactured and distributed highly secretive syrup recipes, bottling and selling it locally.

This was the start of 'business format franchising' as we now know it; offering a turnkey package from franchisor to franchisee in many instances, it was firmly established as a distinct business model and proven system by the 1950s.

The huge growth in this modern system of franchising is attributed to milkshake machine salesman Ray Kroc who, while visiting San Bernardino in California, frequented a popular and busy drive-thru restaurant that had bought his machines – which was owned and run by the McDonald brothers... He opened the first restaurant in their name in Des Plaines, Illinois and purchased the brand outright in 1961.

In the 1950s and 1960s the popularity of franchising really took off, in tandem with huge growths in population, economic output and social change, and began to appear internationally including in the UK for the first time. Catering companies led the way.

Amongst the earliest practitioners in this country was food giant J Lyons & Co., who franchised the hamburger chain Wimpy in 1955 as well as ice-cream brands Lyons Maid and Mr Softee in the 1950s. ServiceMaster, still a huge international franchise business today, began franchising in the UK in 1959. By the mid-1960s some of the largest fast-food brands had become well-established international franchises, led by McDonald's and KFC.

This boom period in franchising was not to last long; by the 1970s franchising in the UK had slowed, partly in response to the faltering economy but more as a result of the damage done to its reputation by non-franchise systems such as pyramid schemes describing themselves as franchises; they were based around the handing over of money for a promised lucrative return on investment, which of course rarely came.

Despite still offering some very real opportunities, franchising was unfairly tarred with the same brush by many and its popularity waned.

Eight of the largest franchise brands in the UK at the time decided they needed to do something to differentiate their own ethical business practices from those companies with bad ones, and as a result in 1977 the British Franchise Association (bfa) was formed. The founding member companies were ServiceMaster, Dyno-Rod, Holiday Inns UK, Kentucky Fried Chicken, Wimpy International, Ziebart GB, Prontaprint and Budget Rent a Car.

With no previous set standards in the UK, the industry thus created its own regulatory body and accredited a company's suitability for membership on strict criteria related to operational practices, business procedures, franchise agreement terms and the support offered to franchisees.

Franchising has since flourished into an industry that now has nearly 1,000 brands in a multitude of different sectors. Long gone are the days when it revolved around cars and catering, and nowadays its eclectic mix of businesses includes everything from hairdressing to photography, pet care to children's sport coaching. Franchising has never been in better health than it is now. The authoritative annual research into the state of the industry, the NatWest/bfa Franchise Survey, has shown both short- and long-term growth trends to be very strong in the sector, including prior to and since the economic downturn in 2008.

From its feudal roots to becoming one of the fastest-growing sectors of the UK economy, franchising has come a long way. With many more people now looking to take charge of their careers and family life by running their own business, it looks set to go a whole lot further in the years to come too.

The section above is reproduced with permission of the British Franchise Association.

Sectors that are franchised

The list of sectors that have had franchised businesses established is virtually endless, and can be divided as many times as you'd like to split various sectors. Broadly speaking, the following sectors are represented within the UK franchise industry:

► Retail

► Food & beverage

► Automotive

► Hotels

► Business-to-business

► Cleaning

► Health & beauty

► Property maintenance

► Leisure & travel

► Printing & signage

► Lettings & estate agency

► Distribution.

Examples of franchises

As you can see from the list above, there is a range of businesses that are franchised, and this is reflected by some of the examples of franchised businesses below (in no particular order):

Apollo Blinds	Jim's Mowing
Arsenal Soccer School	Kumon
Auditel	Little Kickers
Autosmart	MAC Tools
Bairstow Eves	Mail Boxes Etc
Bang & Olufsen	McDonald's
Belvoir Lettings	Minster Cleaning

Boots Opticians	No+Vello
Burger King	O2
Card Connection	Oscar Pet Foods
Chipsaway	Ovenu
Clarks Shoes	Pirtek
Costa Coffee	Post Office
Countrywide Signs	Red Flag Alert
Domino's Pizza	Revive!
Dream Doors	Signs Express
Dyno	Snack-in-the-Box
Energie Gyms	Stagecoach
eTyres	Subway
Home Instead	Total Clean
HomeXperts	Trussell Trust
Interlink Express	Wimpy

What a franchise looks like

Business format franchises can come in all shapes and sizes, and the brands listed above show that these businesses can be either large, consumer-facing retail chains or smaller businesses operated from home. There are, however, a few similarities across most franchise networks that help define the business as a business format franchise:

▶ **The use of a franchisor's brand by a franchisee:** Whether the brand is controlled rigidly, as is the case with the major food and beverage franchises, or the brand is secondary to the community trading name (such as with the Trussell Trust where, for example, franchisees will operate as 'Swindon Foodbank' with a sub-brand of 'seeded by the Trussell Trust'), there will be some element of branding provided from the franchisor to the franchisee. Usually, a franchise will control its brand, and ensure that a franchisee's signage, printed literature and web presence is consistent with the franchise's brand guidelines.

▶ **The use of a franchisor's operating system by a franchisee:**
A franchise agreement includes passing the systems and
processes of the business to the franchisee. Every business
format franchise should be systemized to a point where
the operations can be defined within an operating manual,
which can be passed to anyone to allow them to run the
business. The phrase that is often used for this is a 'turnkey
business'. An incoming franchisee should expect to receive
an operations manual as part of the package.

▶ **Payments from the franchisee to the franchisor:** In exchange
for the brand and systems, there is normally a payment
from the franchisee to the franchisor. This will usually
be both an initial franchise fee, together with an ongoing
management service fee (MSF). The MSF is often calculated
as a percentage of sales; however, in some businesses it is a
flat monthly fee. There are often other fees payable, such as
a contribution to a central marketing levy, or purchases of
centrally supplied goods.

▶ **Legal agreement between the franchisee and franchisor:**
Underpinning the above is a legal agreement between the
franchisee and franchisor. This usually takes a standard
form and is often non-negotiable. A legal agreement
will set out the obligations of both the franchisee and
franchisor, the payments due to the franchisor from
the franchisee, and will set the scene for the ongoing
relationship.

Why does a business franchise?

Although this book is primarily focused on you, the potential
franchisee, I believe that it is important to consider the
franchisor's perspective and the reason why they entered into
franchising as a route to growth for their own business. This
will give you a rounded view on franchising as a concept, and
should help you to understand how most franchisors work.

Key idea: Advice from an expert

Franchising does not necessarily suit every business. It should be considered alongside the more traditional business growth methods, such as organic growth, joint ventures and licensing. In general, companies decide to begin franchising for one of three reasons: lack of money, people or time.

The primary barrier to expansion that today's businesses face is lack of capital; franchising allows companies to expand without the risk of debt or the cost of equity. Since franchisees provide the initial investment at the unit level, franchising allows for expansion with minimal capital investment on the part of the franchisor.

In addition, since it's the franchisee, and not the franchisor, who signs the lease and commits to various service contracts, franchising allows for expansion with virtually no contingent liability, thus greatly reducing a franchisor's risk.

The secondary barrier to expansion is finding and retaining good unit managers. All too often a business owner spends months looking for and training a new manager only to see that manager leave or, worse still, get hired by a competitor.

Franchising allows a business to overcome these problems by substituting a motivated franchisee for a unit manager. Interestingly enough, since the franchisee has both an investment in the unit and a stake in the profits, unit performance will often improve.

Thirdly, opening another location takes time: looking for sites, negotiating leases, securing funding, hiring and training staff. The end result is that the number of units you can open in any given period of time is limited by the amount of time it takes to do it properly.

For companies with too little time (or too few staff), franchising is often the fastest way to grow. That's because it's the franchisee who performs most of these tasks. The franchisor provides the guidance, of course, but the franchisee does the legwork.

Put simply, franchising offers ten important advantages to a business:

▶ **Capital** is provided by the franchisee since they fund the set-up of the business

▶ **Faster growth** is possible – since there is less cost involved, the company can set up units very quickly

▶ **Fewer staff** need to be employed by the head office, since many staff will be managed by the franchisees

▶ It provides a **wider range** and **more secure units** for products and services

▶ The franchisor is **not concerned with the detail** of the day-to-day operation of each unit

▶ The business unit is operated by **highly motivated owners**, as the franchisees reap the benefits of their own hard work

▶ The business benefits from **local knowledge and contacts**

▶ There is **greater protection** against the forces of a recession

▶ A mature franchise network **enables national customers** to be serviced

▶ There is **greater return** on capital invested by franchisor.

Euan Fraser QFP, AMO Consulting

As you would have seen from the examples of franchises given earlier, there is no pre-defined 'type' or 'size' of business that could or should franchise. All that matters is that a business that looks to franchise has a proven and replicable business model, which is profitable and provides a 'win-win' relationship between franchisor and franchisee.

It is important to bear in mind that, particularly in light of the expert comments above, some businesses use a very loose interpretation of business format franchising as a way of expanding without putting their time and money at risk. These businesses might have done it properly; however, it is always worth performing due diligence on any opportunity that you might look at. This is a topic that is covered later in the book.

Focus points

✳ While franchising has been around in various forms for a long time, it is still a relatively new area to many people.

✳ Franchises can be developed in various sectors, and one franchise might be the polar opposite of another – it isn't limited to certain types of business.

✳ Franchises can also be established by relatively new businesses, as well as by long established businesses.

✳ A franchise normally consists of the licence of a brand, system and a 'way of doing things', together with a fee for the rights to those.

✳ The franchisor and franchisee are bound together by a legal agreement.

✳ A business can decide to franchise for a number of reasons, and down the line as a prospective franchisee it is worth understanding why your chosen franchise had originally decided to expand through franchising.

Next step

In this chapter you have learned some of the basics of business format franchising. In the next chapter we will look at why you might decide to invest in a franchise.

2

Why invest in a franchise?

In this chapter you will learn:

▶ *How to compare a franchise investment against other franchises, and other investment opportunities*

▶ *The pros and cons of investing in a franchise*

▶ *What you get for your money when you invest in a franchise*

▶ *The expected financial return from a franchise.*

Now that you know a little about the history of franchising, and what makes a business format franchise, it's now time to look at why you should invest in a franchise. You may have heard that a franchise is 'expensive'; however, to appraise the investment correctly you need to balance the financial risk against the projected return, and weigh up what you get for your money.

It is also important to weigh up the investment against other forms of business startup, since all new businesses require some level of capital injection to get them started; and against other forms of investment. In this chapter we'll also look briefly at the funding market, as this often dictates the level of investment that a potential franchisee can pump into their business.

Comparing a franchise investment against other investments

The first thing to look at when deciding whether a franchise is right for you is to compare the returns that you might get from a franchise versus the returns that you might get from other investments, and indeed versus starting your own business.

Typically, most people look at two things when appraising an investment:

▶ **Investment yield:** this is the return that you receive on a regular basis from your investment. This could be dividends from a shareholding, or rent received on a property. In a business, this is the annual profits that the business makes.

▶ **Capital (asset) growth:** in addition to investment yield, you would typically expect the value of your investment to increase in line with other similar assets. This might be an increase of the share price for a listed company, or an increase in property values for a rental property. For a business, this will be your resale value.

So, when deciding whether to invest in a franchise, you need to look at both the projected 'investment yield' – the profit that the business will make; together with the 'capital growth' – the eventual asset that you will have to sell when you decide to exit the franchise (*see* Part Eight).

Once you have an idea of the potential returns, both from a yield and asset perspective, you can then use these statistics to compare your potential venture against other types of investment, including starting a similar business outside of a franchise model.

The pros and cons of investing in a franchise

There are some very clear advantages and potential disadvantages of investing in a business format franchise:

ADVANTAGES

A proven business model and brand – by joining a franchise, you are obtaining the business model that has been proven to be successful in the past. In the case of established franchise networks, you might also be purchasing a well-known brand, either locally or nationally. To put this into context, a franchisee of McDonald's could open in almost any town across the UK and have brand recognition locally from day one, unlike an independent fast-food startup.

A knowledgeable support team – the franchisor will have an obligation to support you in your business, and as a franchisor becomes more mature they tend to employ regional franchise managers to provide hands-on advice and support. Since the franchisor has a vested interest in your success, particularly if they receive a percentage-based MSF (management service fee), they will be motivated to help you develop your business to generate more sales and ultimately make more profit.

Reduced risk – as mentioned earlier, the business model is proven, and the main benefit of this is that, in theory, the risk to you as an investor should be lower than investing in a startup business. This is simply because there is a proven blueprint (the operations manual), which will give you the benefit of the franchisor's experience in business.

Control over your earning potential – unlike shareholdings in listed companies and rental properties, you will have a direct input into the performance of your business, whether at an operational level (by devoting more hours to doing the work of the business) or at a managerial/strategic level.

DISADVANTAGES

Potential reliance on the franchisee – most business format franchises require a level of input from the franchisee, and hence cannot be deemed true 'turnkey' investments. There is therefore the potential risk of you being unable to work, which will affect the return that you will receive from your business – traditional investments such as shareholdings in listed companies and rental properties will continue to generate a return without your direct input.

Entry costs – a franchise has an entry cost, which is made up of both the franchise fee and the initial working capital, which might appear to be higher than the minimum required investment to start your own business, or indeed the minimum required investment for entry to the stock market.

Restrictions on trade and territories – while trading as a franchise you will be under various obligations that will be set out within the franchise agreement. They will include operational requirements (for example, you may be required to operate at certain times, or restricted to supplying certain products); and also restrictions, particularly if you are given an exclusive territory. These restrictions are generally for the good of the whole network, either from a reputational perspective or from a commercial perspective; however, as an independent business owner you would be able to operate without these concerns.

The funding market

One of the main advantages of investing in a franchise, which has not been touched on above, is the willingness of major banks to support the business model. From their perspective, they can see the reduced risk of a business operated under a franchise model versus the significant risk that they see with general startups.

To put this into context, and depending on the source that you use for the statistics, at least 50 per cent of businesses fail within their first five years (the average term of a franchise agreement). This is a significantly higher failure rate than within the franchise industry. This statistic will undoubtedly be helped by the fact that 97 per cent of franchisees report profitability, according to the NatWest/bfa 2015 Franchise Survey. This is due to the advantages highlighted above, in that you receive the proven blueprint that has worked in several locations before.

This has the benefit to the franchise industry of improved banking terms compared to lending for non-franchised businesses. In general, the banks that have an active appetite to work within the franchise industry will offer 70 per cent of the capital requirement for an established, reputable franchise brand, compared to 50 per cent of the capital requirement for a general business startup. This topic is explored in more detail in Chapter 6.

What do you get for your money?

Each franchise has a different investment level, and in turn each franchise offers a different package to new franchisees. I've seen a variety of offerings, from those networks who provide the bare minimum to get a business started, through to those who attempt to include every single cost that the business may incur in its first year.

As a general rule, I'd expect that a franchisee should receive at least the following:

Licence to use the brand and systems – this is the fundamental 'package' that the franchisee is buying from the franchisor.

Operations manual – any franchise network that has been set up properly should have an operations manual for the franchisee to refer to. This will include the practical day-to-day routines that the franchisee should follow, and is the 'blueprint' referred to above.

Access to operating systems – most franchise networks now have computerized systems to help their franchisees automate part of their business (such as CRM (customer relationship management) systems) and any new franchisee to the network should receive access to these systems as part of their investment.

Marketing material – at the very least, the franchisor should provide logos and template marketing material for any new franchisee to assist them with their launch.

Access to preferred and nominated suppliers – most franchise networks will have a list of preferred suppliers who will provide products and services at a negotiated rate to franchisees.

It's important that you weigh up the package carefully to ensure that you understand what you are getting for your money.

Case study: Wagging Tails

Hilary Coates is a franchisee of Wagging Tails, a dog-walking franchise, and operates in the Swindon territory. She has only recently joined the network, and here provides the background to her selecting a franchise:

'I was told I was accepted as a Wagging Tails franchisee on 19 March 2014 – I remember the exact date as my poor dog was having surgery on his elbows that same day, so there were definitely mixed feelings.

I was very relieved to be told that the franchisor considered me to be an appropriate candidate since I had been a stay-at-home Mum for the previous 20 years and had no recent experience of the workplace. I knew that too many other businesses would not be able to look past that or consider the other life experiences I had as important. My choice had been to stay at home to bring up my children, something that I have no regrets about, but as my children approached the grand old ages of 21 and 18 and I was going through a divorce, I realized that I wanted to do something that would be fulfilling, bring in a wage and allow me to become independent.

I spent weeks wondering what I could do – I have a degree in psychology but have never technically used it (reverse psychology on children probably doesn't count!), and although I have volunteered over the years at playgroups, schools and sports clubs, organizing events and teams,

I have nothing concrete to show for that. Since I have also been at home with my dog for all of his life, I was very worried about what absences of up to four hours at a time (if I was lucky enough to find a job locally) would do to him.

We had moved to several different countries and back again with my ex-husband's work, but, as far as I knew, experiences like that don't count on job applications.

I had come to the conclusion that working for myself had to be the only solution, but without any relevant business experience I knew it would be hard.

Luckily, one morning a plan started to come together: I spotted a rival home dog boarding company's car locally and looked it up – since I was looking for an alternative to kennels for my dog – only to spot the word "franchising". After researching the company and finding that its business model didn't fit with what I wanted, I found other pet franchises and looked into them more carefully.

My brother, a qualified accountant, suggested that I look at the British Franchise Association website for more advice, and I was able to identify a franchise that appeared to suit me down to the ground. Wagging Tails is a member of the bfa and I was able to find a lot of information about the company on its website.

Further contact with the franchisors, as well as established franchisees, convinced me that this was a business model I could believe in and sell to other dog owners, and that I would get a lot of back up and support. Since I would get my own section on a website, a Facebook site that I could contribute to and an email account all set up for me, it seemed obviously the way to go.

I have never regretted my decision as I have found exactly what I needed – a sound proven business model in an industry that is close to my heart, and where hard work is rewarded. I have people I can call upon for advice and assistance, yet still feel in charge of my own destiny... and I can fit in my daily dog walks and be there for my children and my dog!'

Hilary Coates, franchisee of Wagging Tails

Expected return from a franchise

As mentioned above, there are two ways that you can get a return from any investment – investment yield and capital growth. In a franchise, I'd typically expect that a franchisee should be profitable from the second year of trading; although this varies depending on the type of franchise and level of involvement of the franchisee.

When considering the profitability of a franchise it is important that you consider what would be a reasonable salary for somebody doing the 'job' of a franchisee, and reducing the profit by this amount, so that you have an underlying profit figure for the business itself.

Any capital growth is crystallized at the point of exit of the franchise, ideally through a resale to a new franchisee (touched on in Part Eight of this book). A franchise is valued in much the same way as any other business, although often there is a track record of franchise resales in mature networks, meaning that there are comparable businesses to help establish the resale value.

Key idea: Advice from an expert

Franchising is not just about lining the pockets of the franchisor, although some franchisors do seem to think this. In fact it's about building your own business with the help and support of the franchisor. Now when you are looking at buying into a franchise, it really doesn't matter what brand or sector they are in – if you want to turn your business into a management business you can do. This is something that your franchisor will help you with. It really does depend on you, and what I mean by that is when you start releasing yourself from the day-to-day running of the business is when the business has a sell-on value.

If your business relies on you and you alone then to try to sell that on is very difficult: not impossible, but very difficult. The business has to be able to work as a business. Some people think that they have a business, when in fact they have a self-employed job. By this I mean that if they don't go to work then they don't earn any money. A true business on the other hand still makes money even if you are not there all of the time. This can be through online sales or by having staff working for you.

Your franchise at the end of the day is a business under an umbrella. It can create its own value based on how you operate the business. I have seen many single-unit franchised businesses in my time in franchising that are worth a lot of money: yes the brand and sector can help, but it's the franchisee running the business that makes it valuable.

Michael Bohan, Franchise Resales

There is an underlying point here that is worth considering now, even though it probably couldn't be further from your thoughts at the moment. When entering into a franchise agreement, it is worth considering what your exit plan is. This can be determined by a number of things:

▶ desired retirement plan

▶ desired net worth

▶ desired lifestyle choices.

Although it might seem premature to be considering the exit value of your franchise before you have even chosen a franchisor, this is a surefire way of ensuring that you choose the right network for your desired end goals, and also will ensure that every decision you make during the selection process, and indeed while running the franchise, will work towards what you want to achieve in the future.

Focus points

✳ You should always consider a franchise investment in the same way that you would consider any other investment, without letting emotion get in the way.

✳ Buying a franchise allows you to tap into an existing brand which your potential customers may have heard of.

✳ Buying a franchise also gives you a 'blueprint', through the operations manual, of how to run the business successfully.

* On the flip side a franchise has some restrictions, and you will not be free to run the business in the same way that you might be able to run an independent startup.
* Every franchise is different and you will need to appraise the initial package, in particular the support and training, to ensure that you are happy with the investment.
* It's important to remember that a franchise should develop into a saleable asset, so rather than just looking at the ongoing income you should also consider your exit strategy.

Next step

In this chapter we have looked at why you might decide to invest in a franchise. We will focus on what makes a good franchisee in the next chapter.

3

Who makes a good franchisee?

In this chapter you will learn:

► *The expected skill set of a franchisee*
► *The expected behaviours of a franchisee*
► *How a franchisor might profile a franchisee's personality.*

Now that we know broadly what a franchise is, and some of the reasons why you should invest in a franchise, we can look at what personality traits and skills are desirable, or indeed essential, in a franchisee.

You might think at first that the profile of a franchisee is identical to that of a business owner, but this couldn't be further from the truth. In some networks, franchising can be a rather strange hybrid between employment and self-employment in that the franchisee may be expected to perform work themselves, work to the standards set by the franchisor, and perform this work under the control of the operations manual and the franchise agreement (both discussed later). Clearly, this is quite different from the day-to-day life of a startup business owner, who is free to establish the way he or she does things and the brand that is used. Not all networks operate on this basis, and in other networks franchisees are given near autonomy to run their businesses as they see fit; however, regardless of network there will be a level of control and regulation from the franchisor.

This can conflict with the typical personality profile of an entrepreneur, who might feel like a caged tiger with the 'handcuffs' of a franchise agreement and operations manual dictating day-to-day procedures. On the other hand, a typical employee might also struggle, in that they may be used to having direct control, supervision and direction from a superior. Once an 'employee' has purchased a franchise, they often find that they are shocked that work isn't just magically coming to them!

Expected skills

Depending on the network, there will be varying levels of skills required to join a franchise. Again, some of these depend on the type of network that you are looking at. Some brands that I know of will only recruit franchisees who have experience within the sector. This is particularly true of the children's tuition industry; and, for example, a performing arts school might only take on a franchisee who has both experience and an interest in the arts. Some other networks actively discourage those who have experience in doing the work of the franchise from joining, simply because they do not want to inherit skills that might be deemed 'bad habits' when compared to the way that things should be done according to the operations manual.

Regardless of whether industry experience is necessary, there are numerous transferable skills that are desirable to any franchise network, which can be broadly divided between sales skills and management skills.

SALES SKILLS

Whatever the type of network, every successful franchisee is a successful sales person in some shape or form. As alluded to above, some franchisees believe that upon signing the franchise agreement that the phone will magically start ringing and customers will be willingly signing cheques payable to them! The reality is that this isn't the case, and there is a lot of input and effort required to build a franchise, in the same way that an independent business needs a level of 'sweat equity' put into it.

A typical franchise will have a good proportion of the operations of the business systemized, but there is always an element that requires sales skills – whether that be direct selling to customers, or simply selling the concept and vision of what you are doing to your staff.

MANAGEMENT SKILLS

Any franchise requires a level of management skill, whether the franchise is a single operator 'man in a van', or a multi-unit retail franchise. A franchisee will be expected to manage his or her business affairs, use a CRM tool, deal with staff and customers appropriately, and ultimately make good use of time and money. Fortunately, many potential franchisees will have been exposed to some of these areas during their previous employment (bearing in mind that according to the NatWest/bfa Franchise Survey, 74 per cent of franchisees come directly from employment).

Having said that, it is very rare that a previously employed franchisee has had complete exposure and responsibility for all of these areas, and it would be a wise move for any prospective franchisee to perform a self-appraisal on these skills to ensure that they are choosing the right franchisor who can support them in the areas where they might not have had sufficient experience.

Remember this: View from a former franchisor/ franchisee

I have been in and around franchising for ten years, and there has been a number of times that I have asked franchisors what their selection criteria is for great franchisees, and been told 'a cheque book and a pulse...'. Of course without these two key attributes, especially the second one, a franchisee may not be able to proceed with the investment in a franchise; however, there are plenty of other attributes that should be considered to ensure that the best people are recruited into a franchise organization.

As with recruitment in any business, we tend to hire someone on the strength of their skills but fire them on the weakness of their attitude; the approach to franchisee recruitment is no different and having a strategy in place that will enable us to determine the best fit both technically and emotionally will ensure a 'best fit', which is in the interests of both franchisee and franchisor.

How do good franchisors ensure that they are successful in their recruitment approach?

First, a franchisor should define clearly what the role of the franchisee will actually be. It sounds obvious, but if there is a 'job spec' of what is required from them, then you can match the desired skills and personality to the role.

In my opinion, there are three key attributes that will define a successful franchisee:

1 Ability to attract and sell to new customers.

2 Delivery of excellent service, in line with the manual.

3 Long-term relationships with both customers and franchisor.

Market-leading franchisors should be clear about what background and experience their ideal franchisee should have, including technical abilities, qualifications, references and background checks – and they should also be clear about what personality types they are looking for too...

David Holland MBA – CEO of Results Rule OK, former Action Coach CEO (Europe, Middle East and Asia), and former Action Coach franchisee

Expected aptitudes

The expected skill set of a typical franchisee is probably of no surprise to you since it would be similar to that of most new business owners. There is a set of aptitudes that would be desirable as well, and not all of them fit in with the popular view of entrepreneurship, particularly the 'wheeler-dealer' characters on business TV shows and popular sitcoms. Most franchisors do not simply select their franchisees based on a CV and a list of skills; instead, they recruit based on who the person is, and whether they would be a good fit for the network. Some of the expected aptitudes that really help someone fit within the franchisor/franchisee relationship would be as follows:

HONESTY

The franchisor is going into a partnership with you, which involves significant levels of trust and confidence from both sides. The recruitment process is also not a cheap process, and thus they are making a significant investment in time, money and effort with any new franchisee. Therefore, it is likely that their view will be impacted if there are any signs of dishonesty as, in my opinion, dishonesty within a franchise (on either side, franchisor or franchisee) is the biggest root cause of disputes in franchise agreements.

COMPLIANCE

Following on from honesty, franchisors would also be looking to make sure that you would be compliant with their system, and indeed an advocate of it. Although networks encourage ideas and innovation, for brand protection it is essential that the correct process is taken for these so that other franchisees are not affected by the brand being tainted should an idea not be right for the business. Franchisors want franchisees who are happy to follow the proven business model, not those who wish to create their own new business model.

RISK AVERSION

Although the typical perception of a business owner is that of a calculated risk taker, franchisors often would ask that their franchisees do not take risks with their business model. Again, this comes back to compliance, as franchisees are provided with a blueprint of how the business has been successful in the past. Strategic changes to the business should be undertaken by the franchisor, who has an ethical obligation and responsibility to engage with the network and get their buy-in to the future direction of the network.

PEOPLE SKILLS

Not only are franchisees expected to stick to the system, but they are also expected to deal with staff and customers. Regardless of whether the business is consumer facing or business to business, all interactions with external parties are in fact interactions with other people, and as such a basic level of people skills is absolutely vital when it comes to dealing with anyone either inside or outside of the franchise.

There are also some more general business aptitudes required, as highlighted in the feature box below.

Remember this: View from a franchisor

There are certain attributes that franchise owners must have which are common to all business owners:

* **Self-motivation** – you have to be driven and proactive
* **Ambition** – you need vision
* **Determination** – a full and determined effort is essential
* **Commercial acumen** – a good understanding of the basics of business
* **Leadership skills** – if the business employs staff you need to be capable of giving clear direction
* **Communication skills** – having the ability to positively engage and influence
* **Mental fortitude** – able to maintain focus through difficult trading periods as well as the good ones.

When appointing potential franchise owners, a franchisor will look for all of the above, plus a number of additional vital attributes. **Specifically, candidates will usually be required to demonstrate that they are able to conform**. To reiterate, franchise owners must organize, administer and develop the business exactly as the franchisor dictates, using the tools that it provides. For this reason, being prepared to conform is important and it also explains why people with maverick tendencies are rarely suitable franchise owners. Franchise owners will also be expected to display genuine enthusiasm for the business and to show that they share the values upon which the business has been built.

There is good reason to justify these extra attributes. A franchisor is entrusting a person with its brand, its reputation and its method of operating, all of which will have been carefully developed and refined over time. They expect that franchise owners will use those 'assets' to replicate the business and be capable of achieving the same level of success. So, franchisors will grant franchises to people who they feel confident will be compliant brand ambassadors.

Clive Smith, franchisor MagicMan Franchising

Personality types

One of the fundamental things to understand when deciding whether to become a franchisee is your own personality type. In turn, this is also a key factor that the franchisor will look at when deciding whether to recruit you as a franchisee!

Key idea: Advice from an expert

While I can bring expertise as a former franchisor, I am currently a business coach, and help many businesses understand the benefits of personality profiling. There are plenty of personality profiling tools out there, including one that is very simple and straightforward – the DISC Profile. Based on the answers to just 24 questions, this profile measures a person in terms of their levels of:

* **Dominance** – achieves by overcoming opposition, from modest to egocentric
* **Influence** – achieves by influencing or persuading others, from reticent to enthusiastic
* **Steadiness** – ability to work accurately within existing circumstances, from active to passive
* **Compliance** – cooperates with others to carry out a task, from rebellious to perfectionist.

For example, **a great franchisee will need to be someone who values working within a given set of procedures** – so a level of 'Compliance' may be required – someone who comes out as a rebel may not be a perfect fit, for example.

It may be that someone with a high score for 'Steadiness' fits really well in a team environment where consistency, loyalty and patience are key attributes.

When building relationships with customers and being involved in selling, a franchisee may require higher levels of both 'Dominance' and 'Influence' – the ability to build relationships, display enthusiasm and self-assurance are useful personality traits for people involved in the sales process.

Matching a person's personality to the function they are expected to perform gives us an increased degree of predictability when it comes to performance and retention, two key attributes that determine success in franchisee recruitment.

Additionally, **people whose personality fits closely to the work they do will be more productive,** less stressed and likely be more successful than those where there is a mismatch.

Knowing the details regarding the function or job that a franchisee will be undertaking, the franchisor can determine the DISC Profile that best describes the person best suited to the role. The DISC Profile, along with any other system, is of course not foolproof and should be used only as a guide during the recruitment process; it may be that the profile helps define the training and development needs of an individual.

David Holland – CEO of Results Rule OK, former Action Coach CEO (Europe, Middle East and Asia), and former Action Coach franchisee

Focus points

* There is no such thing as a 'typical' franchisee; however, there are certain skills and behaviours that the best performing franchisees share.

* A franchisor will look to profile you based on their desired skills and behaviours to ensure that you have the highest possible chance of success in their network.

* Many franchisors don't actually look for 'on-the-job' skills, since these can be taught. Some actively discourage industry experience in case you have inherited bad habits.

* The right behaviours are a vital area for any franchisor, and they will look to make sure that you are someone that they can entrust with their brand.

* In particular, franchisors will look to make sure that you can follow the system.

* Some franchisors will use personality profiling tools such as DISC. There are no right answers to the questions that these tools pose, and they allow both sides to understand whether granting the franchise is the right option for the franchisor.

Next step

In this chapter we've looked at the expected skills and aptitudes of a franchisee. This will help you understand what a franchisor is looking for from the very first contact. Next up, we will be looking at how to create a shortlist of potential franchises.

Part Two

Shortlisting

4

Where do you start?

In this chapter you will learn:

- ▶ *Where you can find franchise opportunities*
- ▶ *How long the process should take*
- ▶ *The key decisions that you will need to make to shape your shortlist*
- ▶ *Some feedback from existing franchisees.*

In the previous section we discussed the basics of franchising, including some background on what a franchise actually is, and the basic skills and aptitudes that a franchisor might expect from a franchisee.

Once you are satisfied that franchising is a viable option for you, you then need to work out how you are going to shortlist your potential franchises so that you can make an informed choice about the business that you should invest in.

Shortlisting process

Everybody will take a different route into the world of franchising. As franchising is not yet an integral part of our business culture (as it is in, say, the US or Australia), the concept is often discovered as part of a wider search for a business option. Often, this route into franchising as a potential option determines the shortlist process for the prospective franchisee. To generalize, there are the following options to help you start selecting a suitable opportunity.

FRANCHISE EXHIBITIONS

Traditionally, franchise exhibitions have been a great way for franchisors to launch their opportunity, and to find prospective franchisees. Over time the value of these has changed in that there are now fewer attendees at the exhibitions; but those prospective franchisees that do attend currently appear to be more likely to invest than before. In my opinion, franchise exhibitions are a great way for you to meet the people behind the brands that you have shortlisted through other methods, and a useful sanity check for you to see other brands when you are further down the franchise investment process. There are numerous franchise exhibitions in the UK, some of which are endorsed by the British Franchise Association – at these exhibitions the exhibitors are either members of the bfa or accredited to a certain extent for the exhibition. At other exhibitions, it would be valuable to do your due diligence to ensure that you are buying into a reputable brand.

MAGAZINES

There are numerous franchise magazines that showcase a range of franchise opportunities, through case studies, directories and advertisements. As with every other method of shortlisting, make sure that you do your due diligence on the brands. It is also important to differentiate between business format franchises that are advertising in the magazines, and other business opportunities such as multi-level marketing and direct selling schemes. Generally, a business format franchise will require a higher investment, but will offer you much more support along the way.

ONLINE

Finally, there are franchise directories where you can search for franchise opportunities by sector, or by investment level, and request information from the franchisor. Please bear in mind that many franchisors are inundated with 'tick-box tickers' who select an information request from every franchisor in their search, and as such the request is considered to be a colder request than perhaps a personal email or phone call. Having said that, the directories do give you a great chance to obtain information from a variety of franchisors to help you start narrowing your selection.

How long does shortlisting take?

There are no set timescales for shortlisting, so you should spend as long as possible making sure that you select the right franchise for you. The decision to invest in a franchise is life changing, and it is vital that it is life changing for the right reasons! Often, buying a franchise will involve remortgaging a property, using savings, and stretching your own personal comfort zones insofar as skills and work/life commitments.

Another important factor is to ensure that your family is 'onside' with your choices, both in respect of the wider decision to invest in a franchise, but also the investment in the specific franchise once you have built a shortlist. There is nothing more difficult than hearing 'I told you so' after a bad day, and one of the steps that many ethical franchisors take is to interview a prospective franchisee's spouse or life partner to ensure that they will get the support at home as well as from them.

What will shape your shortlist of potential franchises?

There are three main areas that will dictate the shortlist that you will prepare:

▶ The sectors that you are prepared to work and invest in (covered below)

▶ The amount that you can afford to invest (covered in Chapter 5)

▶ The type of franchise that you wish to operate (covered in Chapter 6).

What sector should you choose?

There is a wide variety of sectors available, as you will have seen from the listing in Chapter 1, and it is important to choose a sector that you will be motivated to work within. Even if you intend to purchase a 'management' franchise (described in more detail later in the book), the shortlisting process should help you decide what industries really motivate you to build a business. It might sound hard to believe, but I've certainly noticed that the most successful franchisees are those who have a true passion for their sector and the impact that their business makes, rather than just a passion for the profits.

Case study: Trophy Pet Foods

Taking the first step towards running our own business was a perfectly blended mixture of pure excitement and utter terror. We knew the time was right for us to move away from conventional employment, with its limited opportunities for progression. But what we didn't know was how best to manage the very real risks of starting out on our own. Do we start from scratch, buy an existing business or is there another way? While we were vaguely aware of franchising, our association with this term conjured up images of fast food restaurants and American football teams. How delighted we were when we realized that the range of available franchising opportunities is wonderfully varied and encompassing of all budgets.

We are now just about to start our third year with Trophy Pet Foods, who have been members of the bfa for 18 years. Through them we have found the perfect partner: an outstanding and supportive brand that continues to fuel our enthusiasm but is always there, with the right answers, advice and best practice when we need them. And through franchising we feel that we have come as close as possible to finding the holy grail of work/life balance, freedom and control, while being supported by a world-class brand and the expertise that it can offer.

Matt Snell, franchisee Trophy Pet Foods

Case study: Wagging Tails

I came across the pet care franchising sector because I was looking for an alternative to kennels for my own dog. I had never heard of home boarding as a franchise; I assumed that every home boarder was someone who set up in their own home and took in dogs from different families.

That wouldn't have been suitable for me, as my dog is not happy with other dogs in our house, so I hadn't really considered pet care as an option when I was racking my brain trying to come up with something I could do.

Once I was aware that home boarding could be an option as a franchise, and that it was something I could truly believe in as a 'product', the only issue was deciding which one to go with – there are quite a few out there, but many appeared to be 'too cheap to be true', one was too expensive to genuinely consider, another one had a 'special price' and not many were connected with the bfa.

I wanted to feel that I had protection for myself and that I went with someone who had been advised as to the proper value of their franchise, who was interested in getting the right people, not just someone who had seen a bargain.

Wagging Tails ticked all the boxes for me in those categories and I would advise anyone to do some research and make sure that any franchise they are considering can demonstrate that they have set themselves and their franchisees up for success.

Hilary Coates, franchisee of Wagging Tails

The key takeaway from the above two examples is that the franchisees didn't enter franchising with a preconceived idea of the sector that they were going to work in. In fact, Hilary didn't believe that her chosen industry was a possibility until she had done her research on the various types of businesses that are franchising. The thing that shines through from both examples is the sheer passion that the franchisees have for what they do; and for me that is perhaps the biggest determining factor when considering whether a franchisee will be successful.

Key idea: Advice from an expert

With more than 900 different franchise brands to choose from, deciding on the right franchise for you can feel overwhelming at first. **The place to start when it comes to joining a franchise is with yourself.** The best performing franchisees in any network are the ones that are well matched to the business operation.

That's why self-reflection is crucial – think about your personality, your experience and what you're passionate about. It's not easy to assess yourself, but it's the right place to begin!

Good franchising is all about transferable skills; you do not usually need professional experience in the business sector as the training and support on offer will give you what you need to succeed. Perhaps you excel in sales, at managing people, in building relationships, with practical skills... consider your skill set carefully and consider franchises that play to those strengths.

Combine this with an examination of your personality – do you like working alone, outdoors, leading teams, and so on? All this will give you a strong base from which to explore your options.

Make sure you take note of bfa membership: brands that have put themselves forward to be scrutinized against a strict code of ethics.

And, finally, make sure you're excited and passionate about the business; you need to be motivated each day to work hard on making it a success!

Pip Wilkins, Chief Executive, British Franchise Association

Focus points

* There are a number of places where you can learn about franchise opportunities, and it is worth exploring online, reading the magazines and attending the exhibitions.
* Investing in a franchise is a huge decision – life changing in fact – and so you should allow the right amount of time to make sure that you make the right choice.
* Make sure that your spouse/life partner is happy with your shortlist, to help avoid any potential 'I told you so' conversations.
* Your shortlist can broadly be dictated by the sectors you are prepared to work in, the amount you can invest, and the type of franchise that you want.
* Not all franchised sectors are immediately apparent, so don't enter the shortlisting process with any preconceived ideas.
* Finally, make sure that you are excited and passionate about the opportunity.

Next step

In this chapter we looked at the basics of the shortlisting process, and the factors that can affect or limit your shortlist. Perhaps the most common limitation that I regularly see is finance, and the next chapter will tell you more about how much funding you can achieve, and ultimately how much you can afford.

5

How much can you afford?

In this chapter you will learn:

▶ *How the banks view franchises*
▶ *How much a bank is prepared to lend against a franchise opportunity*
▶ *How franchisors advertise their initial startup costs*
▶ *The difference between the initial franchise fee and the total investment required.*

One of the main criteria when considering a franchise is the affordability of the initial franchise fee and associated costs of getting started in business, such as working capital and any stock or assets required to get started. In my experience this is usually the main limitation that most franchisees have, and plays a huge part in the selection process.

In fact, I'm fairly confident in saying that a vast number of franchisees spend as much as they can afford (through personal funds and external funding), and so being clear on the affordability levels is vital when starting to consider your franchising options.

Understanding the principles of funding

Even before you attempt to gauge how much you can afford it's important that you fully understand the basic principles of external funding, unless you are in the fortunate position of being able to finance the purchase of the franchise from personal funds. Even if you are able to fund the entire startup costs of the franchise personally, it may be desirable to source external funding for a proportion of the costs.

In particular, you should consider both what the banks want to receive from you and how much they would be prepared to fund you in the new venture.

Key idea: Advice from a bank

When thinking of buying a franchise, it is vital to do your research – so make sure you ask the right questions of the franchisor and, particularly, make sure you speak to as many existing franchisees as you can.

Set out your intentions in a well thought through business plan that demonstrates its potential and how you expect to reach your goals. You must be realistic and show you are aware of the challenges and how the business is expected to perform.

Once you have worked out your own financial contribution to your business, it's time to look at what you need to borrow. The business plan should include details about the franchise, the costs, the sector it operates in, the competition (locally, regionally and nationally), your CV, your assets and liabilities, and projected financial information: balance sheet, cash flow and profit & loss for a minimum of two years. If you are buying an existing franchise business the bank is keen to see the actual financial performance figures for this business.

Most banks will lend up to 70 per cent of the total startup costs of a franchise, including any working capital requirement, although this may be nearer to 50 per cent for a less-established franchise concept. Any borrowing under £25k will normally be available unsecured but security will generally be required for anything above this.

You need to ensure that your request for support recognizes both the challenges you face and opportunities available. Those who demonstrate a balanced and informed view of an opportunity tend to have a higher chance of obtaining support from banks because they are able to demonstrate they understand both the rewards and risks. By articulating a plan that shows how you would manage risk within a business, you are instilling confidence and creating a good impression.

Dave Williams, former director (Franchising) at RBS England & Wales/NatWest Scotland (Future Williams & Glyn)

As mentioned above, the general rule of thumb for financing a franchise is that the banks will lend up to 70 per cent of the initial capital requirement for an established, successful franchise brand. Later in the book we will explore the process of obtaining funding in more detail.

Advertising of initial franchise costs

One of the areas where you will need to proceed with caution is in respect of the figures advertised by franchisors as the initial outlay. From a franchisee perspective, this is one of the challenges raised by the fact that the industry is unregulated, with the exception of the Code of Ethics that is voluntarily adopted by all bfa member franchisors.

Section 3.1 of the Code of Ethics of the bfa states:

'Advertising for the recruitment of Individual Franchisees shall be free of ambiguity and misleading statements.'

While this means that any advertising must be free from factual misstatement (such as advertising the franchise fee as £10,000 when it is actually £15,000), it does not dictate how the initial investment should be disclosed (if at all), nor does it state how this figure should be calculated.

What this means to you as a prospective franchisee is that you should consider whether any amounts quoted are for the franchise fee only, franchise fee plus required purchases from the franchisor, or if they include additional working capital/ asset purchase requirements to start trading.

Funding requirements over the initial franchise fee

The working capital requirements of a business depend on many things, not least the type of business that you are running and the nature of cash flows within that business. Broadly, there are two different types of funding required in addition to the initial franchise fee.

ASSET FUNDING

For most franchises, particularly those outside of the home-based, business-to-business sector, there will be a requirement to purchase some assets. This requirement might simply be for an initial stock of items (for example, a football tuition franchise might be required to purchase only some footballs and children's football kits); however, this will often be a wider-ranging requirement. Depending on the type of sector, you may well be required to fund the purchase of items such as shop fittings, kitchen equipment, vans, tools, and computer systems.

WORKING CAPITAL REQUIREMENTS

The other funding requirement beyond the initial franchise fee is working capital. Every business has some form of working capital requirement, which simply enables it to fund the time between work starting and the customer paying for the completion of the work. The working capital requirements can be established from a business plan, and will form part of the funding requirement of the business.

Payback period

One of the things that you should consider when looking at affordability, and ultimately appraising the investment, is the payback period for the franchise investment. While the payback period varies depending on the type of franchise, the level of head office support, and most importantly the input that you put into the business, it is a metric that you need to consider, based on the network that you are looking at and other similar networks insofar as size of business and type of operation. Generally speaking, the payback period on a management franchise would be longer than the payback on an owner-operator franchise (see the next chapter for more detail on the differences between these two types of franchise), since you – the franchisee – are effectively subsidising the business for the cost of labour for actually 'doing the job'.

Since this period can vary from franchise to franchise, and can ultimately be dramatically affected by your own business performance, I wouldn't get too hung up on this statistic; however, I certainly would look to acknowledge this within your projections and be aware of the target for your investment to be paid back.

Personal risk appetite

Another area that you need to consider is your appetite for risk. As mentioned in the 'Key idea: Advice from a bank' above, the banks want to see that you have taken an impartial and informed view of the risk of the business – and perhaps more importantly they want to make sure that you share the risk with them! Every funder will be looking for you to have some 'skin in the game', and this would ordinarily be through a combination of personal funding, security over assets, and the right balance of motivation to grow the business.

On the face of it, a larger investment will have a larger risk attached since the security over personal assets and the initial capital requirement from you personally will be greater. You also need to consider the risk of the franchise itself – for example, clearly an investment in a well-established, successful brand such as McDonald's, although higher in terms of pounds invested, should be a safer bet than a 'franchise' that hasn't been set up properly, nor tested through a pilot operation. Only you will be able to decide the right level of risk that you are happy to accept, and again it comes back to the key skill of separating your emotions from the logic of deciding whether to purchase the franchise.

Key idea: Advice from an expert

I have been involved within the franchise community since 1988 and worked with some very successful franchisees. These have taken on a franchisor's concept and system and used it very effectively within the franchisor's network to develop substantial businesses. I have also, unfortunately, met others who have not been so successful for one reason or another.

What is interesting is that the reasons for these successes (or not) can be distilled into a very few key points. By taking a little additional time at the outset and resisting the temptation to go with your first option or desire it is possible to reduce the risk element in buying a franchise. By following some simple guidelines, you can make sure that the business you are taking on is the one that is right for you and that will enable you to be successful. Occasionally, 'gut feeling' can pay off but in reality a considered planned approach is much more likely to achieve success.

I hope you will find the following tips helpful:

Decide on your investment level and stick to it

Don't overspend. Invest to the level you can afford. Always include some negative 'what if' planning in your calculations and keep some money back for the unexpected events that may come along later – the unexpected does happen in business. Naturally there must be a balance between recklessness and excessive caution but a business venture is an investment, just don't overspend or overcommit at the start.

Match your income requirement to your investment

While the dream opportunity is to be able to invest £10 and earn £100,000, reality isn't like that. It is important to ensure the franchise you are looking at can realistically provide you with the income you require

within its normal operating parameters. You can usu
large levels of income with a large level of investment
more modest income, however, can be achieved with mu
up front and it is here that a lifestyle choice can be made.

Check the franchisor's projections – are they based on actua
figures or are they just potential earnings?

Ideally, the projections provided to you by the franchisor will represent the average performance for all the existing franchises in their network. Some franchisors, however, may provide only the top performers' results, while others may try to illustrate what could or should be attained. Make sure you know what the figures that are being presented actually represent and that you understand how they fit with the reality of the network's performance.

You just need to be aware what the projections mean, where they have come from and be comfortable that you are able to generate them using the franchisor's system.

Derrick Simpson, former franchisor and former director,
Franchise Resales

Focus points

* The key limitation for most franchisees is the amount of money that they can invest in a franchise.
* Banks take a preferential view on franchising, often funding up to 70 per cent of the total investment for a well-established, reputable franchise.
* It is important that you follow the process for obtaining franchise funding and don't simply speak to a local bank manager. This is covered in more detail in Chapter 13.
* You need to make sure that you are clear on the total investment required, not just the franchise fee. It is also worth establishing how this is made up.
* You need to weigh up how much income you need from the franchise, and whether it is sufficient to meet your needs.
* You also need to consider your risk appetite, since early stage franchises can be riskier than well-established models.

ext step

In this chapter we've looked at the affordability of a franchise – in particular the amount that you can borrow – and how to understand the total amount required. Next, we will look at the different types of franchise available.

6

What sort of franchise should you choose?

In this chapter you will learn:

▶ *The difference between management and operational franchises*

▶ *What territories are and how a franchisor decides on what area to allocate*

▶ *What 'area developer' and 'master franchise' agreements are.*

One of the first choices that you need to make when selecting a franchise is deciding what sort of franchise you want to purchase. As you will have seen from the introduction in Chapter 1, there are various sectors in which businesses franchise, and these sectors comprise businesses of all different shapes and sizes. Perhaps the biggest differentiator between types of franchise is the split between **management** and **operational** franchises.

Do you need industry experience?

In a word, 'no'. However, there are exceptions to this! The purpose of a franchise is to provide an investor with a business model that will allow him or her to generate an ongoing profit, and to provide a saleable business at the end of the franchise term. In order to provide this opportunity to as many prospective franchisees as possible, most franchisors systemize their businesses to the point where every process is documented in their operations manual.

As stated above, the devil is in the detail with questions like this. Some franchisors actively discourage those with industry experience, as bad habits picked up over years of experience can be detrimental to the overall network. Also, experienced individuals are more likely to challenge the system, which might not be what the franchisor wants. There are some operational (and indeed management) franchises where industry experience is absolutely essential. For example, children's tuition businesses are best operated by those who have both experience and an interest in the subject taught, and this experience removes a significant amount of training from the onboarding time required for each new franchisee.

Regardless of any requirement for industry experience, a franchisor will always be looking for transferable skills and experience when evaluating a new franchisee in areas such as management and sales.

Management vs operational franchises

One of the potential franchisee's biggest decisions is whether to invest in a management franchise or an operational franchise.

Understanding and honestly appraising your own strengths and weaknesses will help you decide what is right for you, and in most cases your available funding will also dictate the types of franchise that you can invest in.

Key idea: Advice from an expert

When you're looking at whether to choose a 'man in a van' or a management franchise you'll have to be brutally honest with yourself. The most important thing is that you know who you are: what you enjoy, what you're good at and what you're poor at.

If you enjoy being 'on the tools' and working in the business delivering the end service or product then a 'man in a van' franchise is right for you. You'll be the operator of the whole business – meeting the customers face to face and being actively involved in the day-to-day work. You'll come to expect long days because the paperwork still needs to be done when you're finished with your customers and that usually won't be until you get home. However, you are in charge – you don't report to a boss. You are in control of your own destiny – but that destiny is limited by the number of hours in a week.

A management franchise is different. It enables you to be the owner and not the operator of the business. For example, if you run a cleaning franchise the business requires you to be a business-focused manager and not a cleaner.

As well as being less physically hands-on, the most obvious benefit of a management franchise is that it provides a framework for you to build a much larger and more profitable business.

Management franchisees are generally responsible for all the management aspects of the business: hiring and managing staff, looking after the money and paying the bills, dealing with customer enquiries, organizing marketing campaigns, distributing leaflets and, most importantly, seeking new business. Strong leadership skills are vital as you'll need to enthuse, train and encourage your staff so that they deliver your services with excellence. There's much more responsibility and a greater investment in a management franchise but there's also greater potential to build a substantial business.

Euan Fraser, QFP, AMO Consulting

Remember that one of the key differences between an operational franchise and a management franchise is the payback period, as alluded to in the last chapter. I would always expect a 'man in a van' franchise to generate a profit sooner than a management franchise; however, the longer-term profitability will probably be lower. Another related factor to consider is the resale value of the franchise. In my experience, it is far easier to sell a business that doesn't depend on the owner, than it is to sell a job!

Territories, and the size and scope of a franchise

Once you are clear on whether you would prefer a management or an operational franchise, you can then consider the projected size of the business that you would like to invest in. As a general rule, operational franchises will have much lower potential than a management franchise; however, not all management franchises are the same.

The potential size of your franchise will be dictated by the territory that you are allocated, the initial working capital funding that you can generate, and the appetite of the franchisor towards multi-unit owners.

There is an oft-quoted saying that 'one plus one equals one and a half' in franchising, in respect of franchisees purchasing a neighbouring territory. This reflects the dilution of an operational franchisee's efforts once they have another area to manage. This saying is based on the franchisor's experiences, but you also have to consider your own profitability as well – unless you are situated on the borders of your first and second territories, it is likely that you will have more running costs and spend proportionally more time travelling than before.

Key idea: Advice from an expert

In a large number of franchise models your territory will at some point place itself at the centre of a conversation between you and the franchisor.

A territory usually grants some degree of exclusivity in a given geographical area to you. For example, the franchisor may be committing not to set up another franchise within the defined area, or may allow you sole rights to marketing within that area. Regardless of the type of exclusivity granted, it will have an impact on how and where your business operates.

This makes it imperative that you take the time to research how the franchisor has decided upon the territory that is being granted to you, regardless of their perceived success.

The franchisor may have employed the services of a third party to create the territory network on their behalf or have undertaken the work themselves. Regardless, and ideally, an analysis of the original business and any existing franchisees' operations should have been performed to determine a model that describes the market composition and size required to build a successful business. This model should then have been replicated to create other territories – including yours.

Where driving is involved, it is important that the territory is operationally sensible within the business model. Your profit margin will decrease if you have too far to travel.

The franchisor should be able to confidently demonstrate this, and provide up-to-date demographics that are relevant to the business model, and describe the market size and spread within the territory along with a map to provide a visual aid. If they cannot, ask why. Remember, this is your investment.

Territories mark some form of boundary, the very definition of which describes a limitation. **It is important, however, not to see the territory as a limit to your success** and understand the benefits that are to be had.

First and foremost, **your territory proves the existence of a viable and operationally sensible market**, the composition and size of which has been proven to allow other businesses to flourish and therefore should allow you the same.

Secondly, some degree of **exclusivity helps prevent other franchisees within the same model from cannibalizing your market**, and likewise you theirs. This contributes to a more harmonious franchise network which works together for everyone's benefit.

Some management franchises offer a **cluster model**, whereby the franchisee commits to opening a certain number of outlets within a pre-defined period of time. I've seen these in food and beverage concepts, such as Costa Coffee, and they allow the network to grow rapidly. The downside to these arrangements is the initial investment required from the franchisee to fund this growth, and as such these franchises tend to be at the upper end of the investment range. In truth, these types of franchise agreements also require a very different type of franchisee from most of the opportunities available to you.

Cluster models aren't the only types of franchise that require different skillsets and investment levels. There are other types of agreements that require the franchisee to develop a large area, perhaps even a whole country or region, which can be broadly defined as follows.

Area developer agreements

An **area developer agreement** is often offered for a large area, or sometimes an entire country, to allow a franchisee to build the presence of the brand within a defined territory. These agreements are usually with an international franchisor, and will require significantly more investment than for a normal territory due to the potential scope, and the capital requirements of building the brand.

Area developer agreements do not usually allow for sub-franchising, and as such the area developer is effectively a direct franchisee, just with a larger territory and higher expectations of success. In my experience, though, the terminology used by franchisors and advisers can differ, and in fact some large networks do permit sub-franchising within these agreements. Often, area developer agreements are granted to franchisees in large urban areas such as London, and given the investment levels required these are usually granted to experienced operators.

Master franchises

A **master franchise** is generally offered for an entire country, and these differ from an area developer agreement in that the master franchisee *can* sub-franchise the business. Because of this, the capital requirements are lower since the master franchisee is not expected to fund the growth of the units themselves, and instead recruits for franchisees in the same way that a domestic franchisor would. Before sub-franchising, it is expected that the master franchisee operates a pilot franchise, to test the concept within the country. This is due to the subtle, and not so subtle, differences in business between nations – for example, although the UK and US share a common language, the business customs, the culture and the demographics of the two nations are very different.

In the same way that there are differences between domestic franchisors insofar as the control exerted over the franchisees, I've noticed that there are substantial differences in the approach to business from international franchisors that offer master licences. Some are very 'hands off', and simply allow the master franchisee to operate as the best practice dictates in their home nation; whereas other brands exert significant control over the marketing material, launch, and even legal agreements between them and their franchisees (I know of more than one model where the agreements between the master franchisee and the franchisee are drafted by overseas advisers who have no experience of UK law). There are also several examples of badly translated websites from the home nation, and other areas where due consideration of the UK market hasn't taken place.

It is vital to consider the different requirements in experience and skillsets between an area developer and a master. Effectively, when a master franchise is granted, the master becomes a franchisor and is therefore required to focus on the recruitment and retention of franchisees; whereas an area developer will typically be required to focus on the management of the company-owned locations. At either of these levels of investment, the franchisor would be expecting you to have the ability and experience to hit the ground running and scale the business effectively.

Case study: Social care master franchise

Ken Deary was a very successful McDonald's franchisee between 1994 and late 2005, owning several stores and winning numerous awards, including the British Franchise Association 'Franchisee of the Year' 2002 and McDonald's 'Golden Arches Award' given to the top 30 McDonald's franchisees worldwide. So what would make a very successful franchisee with the best-known franchise brand in the world make the move from franchisee to franchisor?

Deary explains: 'McDonald's is a fabulous brand with fantastic systems and great people, both corporate and franchisees, and I had 11 fantastic years with them, but personally I needed two things in my business life that I just couldn't achieve as a franchisee, even with this superb brand.

First, I needed a business where I felt I could make a difference every day and, second, I felt I had come to the stage in life where I wanted the major challenge of setting up a new business from scratch, while having the potential and scalability to turn it into a national brand in a relatively short timescale.

Finding the right business sector where I could make a difference everyday was the easy part of the equation and where better than social care to make such a difference, delivering care with empathy to vulnerable adults in the comfort of their own home? The second part was the bigger challenge, that is, how do you set up a new business from scratch and make it a national brand within a relatively short timescale? The answer was to buy a master franchise, which with the right opportunity can be a very cost-effective way to build a national business quicker than starting from scratch.'

In 2009, Deary bought the master licence to the US brand Right at Home, a company delivering quality care for vulnerable adults in their own home. The pilot UK operation began in early 2010 and Right at Home has become a national successful brand in the UK social care market within a relatively short timescale.

So what tips are there for investing in a master franchise as a cost-effective way of building a potential national brand?

Remember this: View from a master franchisee

First, **you should choose a proven brand that has seen success elsewhere** so you have a head start in terms of knowing the concept works and has established systems and software that you can adapt locally and, importantly, gives you the credibility of being part of an international network when speaking to potential franchisees. **Ensure the model will work in the UK first by running a pilot operation** and ensure you negotiate a realistic price for the master franchise that you pay in stages reflecting the success of new location openings. Bargain hard on initial fees and management service fees; I would suggest using an experienced franchise consultant to help you arrive at a realistic price and payment structure since overpaying for a master franchise can cost you dearly both in terms of cash to develop the business and your future relationship with the franchisor regarding perceived value for money.

Second, **a master franchise should be a model that has been proven to work financially**. Ensure you use an experienced franchise accountant who works with and understands the master franchise model in detail to validate that the model stacks up financially in terms of both upfront master licence fee and ongoing management service fees that will deliver the return on investment you require from the business. Remember to be realistic in regard to your projections and anticipated return on investment. **This is a long-term relationship, therefore ensure you complete the necessary due diligence** required to make you comfortable with the agreement in the long term.

Third, **there should be systems and procedures in place that will save you a lot of time and energy, as opposed to setting them up from scratch**. Understand what systems you are getting in order that there are no surprises and be sure that it will take minimum adaptation for the UK market in order to ensure full value for your money.

A final word of advice: **you are entering a legally binding contract and business relationship**. Make sure that you are comfortable with the business and personal relationship and that you have the necessary independence you require to run the day-to-day operations in the manner you want while remembering you are part of an international network or brand. You need to be comfortable giving up a certain degree of independence in return for buying the **intellectual property** an established franchisor can give you. In a nutshell, are you comfortable with the balance?

Ken Deary, Master Franchisee, Right at Home

As you can see from the above case study and franchisee advice, franchises truly do come in all shapes and sizes – you can take on a franchise agreement for a very small territory that you would work in yourself, through to a master licence for an entire region of several countries. Perhaps the main thing to remember is that you need to ensure that you are comfortable with what you are taking on, insofar as your own personal suitability for the role that you will be undertaking, but also whether the franchise will help you reach your own goals.

Focus points

✽ In most franchises, you will not need direct industry experience – although bear in mind that you would need the expected skills and behaviours included in Chapter 3.

✽ You do need to decide whether you want a franchise where you are actively involved in the day-to-day operations, or whether you would prefer a franchise where you actively manage a team to run the business.

✽ Before investing in a franchise you need to clearly understand the territory you are allocated, decide whether it is sufficient for you to operate your business successfully, and be clear on what you can and cannot do with regards to your operating location.

✽ There are various options available should you wish to invest in a larger opportunity, such as a 'cluster model', an 'area developer' agreement, or a 'master franchise' agreement.

✽ In each of the above agreements you will have a different level of involvement, and a different level of capital requirement.

✽ It is worth engaging an experienced consultant to help you source the right opportunity should you wish to purchase a larger opportunity. There are also specialist events that will provide you with the opportunity to meet some brands that are looking for such franchisees.

Next step

In this chapter you have learned more about the different types of franchises, and in particular the difference between 'driving the van' and 'running the business'. This, together with the understanding of the financial limitations that you may be under, will help prepare you for the next chapter, which will explore in further detail how you can find franchises that meet your criteria.

Part Three

Selecting a franchise

7

Where do you find franchises and how do you create a shortlist?

In this chapter you will learn:

- ▶ *Details of exactly where to look for franchises*
- ▶ *Some practical advice from those on the other side!*

Researching and selecting a suitable franchise can be an arduous task, as not only do you need to build and refine your shortlist, you also need to then step away from the desk to undertake face-to-face conversations and visits to make sure that you are entirely happy with the business that you are looking to invest in.

In this section I've asked a number of my colleagues, both advisers and franchisors, to give you some tips on this process, and how best to approach franchisors. The case studies and quotes should, hopefully, help arm you for the franchise recruitment process, which can sometimes take up to six months.

Expert advice

We'll start with some guidance on where the best places to start looking are.

Key idea: Advice from an expert

People just like you discover franchising via numerous routes: it could be an advert or an article in your daily newspaper; or via an acquaintance, a franchisee you know; maybe you have used a franchised service or outlet; or you may actually have visited a franchise exhibition with a friend and become interested yourself.

Is big beautiful?

As a prospective franchisee, will you only look at the biggest, most colourful ads because these 'obviously' represent a company willing to invest their money in attracting the right person? Or will you look at the small ads, since this 'obviously' reveals companies who are careful and prudent with their money, and will invest it carefully all of the time?

As a potential franchisee, what do you actually see when you first spot a franchisee recruitment advert in a newsprint franchise section or in one of the specialist franchise magazines? Well, a wide variety of adverts for a start! Some will naturally appear more attractive to you than others, but which ones are offering the best franchise opportunity? Is it the slick, well-designed corporate-looking quarter page – the one representing a name you recognize from everyday life or a new brand name – or is it the simple lineage advert?

The simple answer is that a very small proportion of all these assumptions are true. So what should you do?

Write your franchise CV

We are not a franchise consultancy, but we do have more than 40 years of combined experience in the franchise industry, so we know what our franchisor clients are looking for in a prospective franchisee. It is therefore essential that franchise seekers, like you, know what you are looking for in a franchise and writing your personal 'Franchise CV' will help you to focus on franchise opportunities that fit your goals, interests and skillset. If you do not feel confident enough to do this for yourself, a franchisee recruitment specialist or a franchise consultant can be of invaluable assistance. A good consultant does not charge you for their services as they are paid a success fee by the franchisors they find franchisees for.

If you decide you can find the right franchise on your own, what are your research options:

1 *The Franchise Media Marketplace*

What publications or websites will you be looking at?

Depending on what stage of your franchise journey you have reached, you may not yet have discovered the niche franchise media sector, but you probably still have a favourite daily or Sunday newspaper. If you are a regular *Sunday Times* and/or *Times* reader, for example, you will know that the majority of 'business opportunity/franchise' advertisers run lineage adverts.

The franchise specific magazines that are currently available include:

Franchise World – this is the UK's longest-running franchise magazine and is a subscription-only publication; however, it is also distributed at various franchise exhibitions throughout the year. More information can be found here: www.franchiseworld.co.uk where you can also view back issues and the current issue.

What Franchise – this magazine is published five times a year and is part of a large publishing house (Aceville Publications) that also publishes *Making Money*, a monthly franchise and business opportunity magazine and *Global Franchise*, which offers you the opportunity to 'get in on the ground floor' with international franchises expanding into the UK (and other parts of the world). These magazines are all available via WHSmith and via subscription.

What Franchise is also available at a number of retail outlets, conferences, departure lounges and in and around all the franchise exhibitions throughout the year. *Making Money* is also distributed via the same routes as *What Franchise* but with additional exposure at the New Start (see below) & Prysm business expos during the year.

Business Franchise Magazine – this is published ten times a year (July/August & December/January being its two combined issues). The magazine is the official magazine of the bfa (British Franchise Association) and media platform/show guide for the VMG (see below) franchise exhibitions. Information on these can be found here: www.franchiseinfo.co.uk/ and back and current issues of the magazine can be found here: www.businessfranchise.com although, like the other magazines, you can also get it on subscription via the website and sample it at the VMG exhibitions.

Elite Franchise – this is the most recent addition to the franchise media marketplace and further information is available here: www.elitefranchisemagazine.co.uk

2 *The online franchise marketplace*

Ah! the wonderful World Wide Web... we all go there for a variety of reasons and it can provide you and other potential franchisees with a wealth of research materials to aid your search.

There is a plethora of franchise sales websites, just search for 'franchises', 'franchise opportunities' or similar and you will find them in abundance.

3 *Franchise & business-to-business exhibitions*

Whether you are looking for a 'hands-on' or 'white collar' style franchise the likelihood is that you will find a fair selection of all types of franchise at one of the many franchise exhibitions throughout the year which are organized by VMG (www.venturemarketinggroup.co.uk/exhibitions.html) or by New Start Exhibitions (www.newstartexhibitions.com).

Of enormous benefit to those of you who are actually looking to start or grow an existing business, visit 'The Business Show' exhibitions (www.prysmgroup.com).

As you can see from the above, there are several places where you can start your search for franchise opportunities. You'll remember from previous chapters that it is important that you keep an open mind on the sectors that you can work in: not all franchisors are looking for industry experience, but they certainly are looking for the right person, the right skillset and the right attitude.

It might be stating the obvious but it is also important that you are motivated to become passionate about the business that you will be working in. Clearly you wouldn't invest in a franchise that you are opposed to for ethical or religious reasons (for example, not many vegans would be keen on investing in a steakhouse), but aside from these reasons it is also important that the franchise keeps you motivated – you need a reason to get out of bed every day for your business, otherwise it is almost certainly destined to fail.

Key idea: Advice from an expert

Research the marketplace for the business you are considering

The Internet provides countless pages of information on virtually everything, so ensure you have looked thoroughly at the business environment and marketplace for the business you are considering. Look for cyclical trends, market saturation, regulatory changes and market intelligence. Undertake research into the franchise, speaking with existing franchisees. An external industry investigation may take an additional few days but balance this against the expense of getting it wrong and you will see the wisdom of this approach.

Play to your strengths

Different types of franchise require differing skills. Some are direct sales based, some are retail services, while others may have a consultancy approach. All, however, require an understanding of finance in some shape or form. Ensure you match your skillset and personality to the style of business you are investigating. Please also remember that just about any business requires the owners to have sales development and people skills – that's what makes the business world go around.

Plan your long-term goals at the outset

Part of planning for a franchise should be to establish your eventual exit route. Consider what the final goal for your business is: whether to sell up and go; take on a partner who will buy you out over time; pass it to an offspring; or even run it until you drop! Each option will have an effect on how you structure your business plan at the outset. Start out with your final goal in mind – that way you will have a good chance of achieving it.

Simple is good

A business that is simple to operate, with structured systems, will be easier to run than one with nebulous concepts where you are left to your own devices to drive it forward. A simple business will also be easier to sell on to a new owner when the time comes for your exit for exactly the same reason – it will be more attractive to a purchaser.

Consider an existing business (a franchise resale) instead of a new startup

Existing businesses will give you that vital cash flow from day one. There is brand presence in the local marketplace and, if appropriate, premises in place and staff who know how to operate the business. A franchise resale may cost a little more but the benefits accrued will usually outweigh the additional cost.

bfa membership

While not being a guarantee against all risks, a franchisor who is a member of the British Franchise Association has gone through a thorough vetting process to attain the standards required by the bfa and should, in theory, adhere to the bfa policies for ethical franchise operations. That doesn't mean you can dispense with the other checks, but it is a good place to start.

Don't talk to negative people!

For me this is an important point. You are going into business with your money, your effort and at your risk. To be successful in business you need to be constantly positive and forward looking. Stay away from negative people who drain your self-confidence and cast doubts on your dreams, efforts and abilities. This world has a tendency to the negative and 'half empty' mindsets; remember it is you who every morning has to drive your business, you who will motivate your staff and you who will reap the rewards of success – don't let others take that away from you with negativity and bad advice.

**Derrick Simpson, former franchisor and former director,
Franchise Resales**

Franchisor case studies

Case study: British Franchise Association

When franchisors and franchisees work together it is hard to find a more successful business model. **However, the franchise industry is no different from any other sector: you will find good, bad and ugly franchisors.**

The trick as a prospective franchisee is to find the good ones before investing your money. This can only be done by comprehensive due diligence and research.

A good place to start is to look at franchisors who are members of the British Franchise Association (bfa), a list of which can be found on the organization's website. The bfa promotes ethical franchising within the UK, and in order to join a franchisor must satisfy a strict accreditation process that evaluates its model.

That assessment includes evidence of financial viability and sustainability, a review of the franchise agreement and that practices comply with the European Code of Ethics for Franchising. Membership of the bfa ensures that a franchisor runs an ethical and successful business and should be an important part of any prospective franchisee's research – but only a part of it.

It always surprises me that people are willing to invest their money in a franchise before ever travelling to see the franchisor's office facilities. Visiting the head office and meeting the team will give you a good idea of how the franchisor runs its company and supports its franchisees. A good franchisor will welcome visitors, is proud of its successful franchisees and will be happy for you to meet and speak with employees as well as members of its network.

Assessing the support on offer to help franchisees build a successful business is critical. The best way to do this is by talking to a cross-section of its franchisees – the people who are where you might be in time and can share their experiences of life in the network. Make sure you have a plan of what you want to find out, and ask the same questions of each so you can assess how different franchisees feel about the same aspects of the business.

The key things to learn include:

* What training does the franchisor offer, both initially and ongoing?
* How well supported do the franchisees feel?
* How does the franchisor develop the system and introduce new policies and products?
* What quality control is done by the franchisor?
* Does the franchisor encourage the network to share best practice and experiences with each other?

In addition, existing franchisees can inform you if the financial projections you're given are achievable. Talk to a range if you can – newer and more established – to get a range of views and experiences.

Any franchisor worth your time and money is open, honest and transparent. Asking questions, meeting the team and speaking to existing franchisees should all be welcomed by any ethical operator.

At the end of your research, if you understand why the franchisor uses franchising as a business model, if you have a good idea of the support available and if you have a feeling that the franchisor and its network of franchisees strive together to be successful, then you have probably found a good one.

Simon Bartholomew, Chairman of the British Franchise Association and franchisor, Oscar Pet Foods

Case study: Wilkins Chimney Sweep

So the first thing we discuss when recruiting is 'what do you know about franchising?' We want to find out whether the person in front of us is simply excited at the thought of being a chimney sweep (yes – believe it or not there are many who fall in love with the idea!) or whether that person is excited at the prospect of being a fully supported business owner in what happens to be a chimney-sweeping business. That differentiation is quite difficult to make as it can be very subtle – but we believe that it's incumbent upon us to make sure that the candidate knows what it is that they are getting involved with.

If a prospect has been on a bfa 'Prospective Franchisee' seminar we feel that they are starting from a good place – despite the endless questions that they bring to the table, we love them! The point is that this is someone who gets the deal – who realizes that they are making a commitment – albeit one that may only be six years in our case – but still a commitment. And that research means they also bring good thinking with them – a mind that seeks to understand fully – and if they have been paying attention they realize that there is a relationship to be built: that the franchisor has as much to gain from taking the right franchisees as the franchisees have from joining the franchise that is right for them.

We have the advantage of being quite a 'simple' model. Our franchisees 'do what it says on the tin'.

We don't have to spend a lot of time explaining the basic functionality of the business but we do spend a fair bit of time driving home that this is a business. Only those people who invest time and energy will even begin to grow that business. We need prospects to hear, and understand, that we have a model that we know works but that they need to look at some key indicators for themselves (fitness levels, enthusiasm, basic technical skills) and for the area (the need for the service!) because they need to be comfortable, as do we, that they have the correct aptitudes and attitude, and that they are in a business where they can be utilized. We expect people to spend some time answering guided questions in a business plan.

In the past, we've had very half-hearted business plans presented to us. To be fair we could send these back to be re-done – but why would we? The person presenting them has taken no pride and made no commitment to looking properly at the opportunity – this does not bode well. We don't ask for an easy ride – we are committed to supporting our franchisees with anything and everything that we can – but we only want to do that for people who engage, enthuse, appreciate and drive their own business in their own territory.

There are franchisors who say they 'award' territories. I understand this thought process but while we are a bit picky, we believe that we create a partnership because both parties have something that the other wants! We could not expand our business without the franchisee. They could not hope to drive as quick a start, as fine a brand, such tested marketing practice, or such established back office practices that allow a franchisee to build a business that they can ultimately sell without us. They could be chimney sweeps. But not necessarily run good, ethical, sustainable and solid businesses.

Our recruitment process is simple. We provide some information. The prospects like what they read. They come to a meeting where we talk a lot and they talk a little. They like what they've heard. They come to another meeting when they talk a lot and we talk a little. Our best recruitment interviews at this point are those where the prospect comes back after finding out about us with a list of questions ranging from practical (what do I wear?) to bold (can I be successful?) to incisive (how do I look more closely at MY territory to make sure it will sustain a good business?). But we also like the very challenging: 'One of your franchisees didn't make it. Why? What went wrong?' We know that they know things go wrong and really want to hear that we have learned from this – that we shoulder some of the blame – that we care enough to be open.

We often have other franchisors suggest we're a bit fussy. We are. We've made a few mistakes and we've learned from them. We know from some really established franchisors that mistakes will always happen. But if you, as a prospective franchisee, think carefully about this – it works: we are trying to build a group of people who want to run a successful business. We have their best interests at heart because in building that group we can build the network bigger, stronger and offer more to the people who join it. And if it's not too crass, we'll all make money! This is, after all, the point...

Louise Harris, franchisor Wilkins Chimney Sweep

Websites and online directories

www.whichfranchise.com

www.franchisedirect.co.uk

www.franchiseinfo.co.uk

www.selectyourfranchise.com

www.franchisesales.co.uk

www.workingmums.co.uk/franchise-opportunities

uk.businessesforsale.com/uk/franchises

www.daltonsbusiness.com/franchises-for-sale

www.totalfranchise.co.uk

Magazines

What Franchise www.what-franchise.com

Making Money www.makingmoneymagazine.com

Global Franchise www.globalfranchisemagazine.com

Franchise World www.franchiseworld.co.uk

Business Franchise www.businessfranchise.com

Elite Franchise www.elitefranchisemagazine.co.uk

Exhibitions

The National Franchise Exhibition (usually mid-February, and late September/early October, NEC, Birmingham)

The British & International Franchise Exhibition (usually mid-March, Olympia, London)

The British Franchise Exhibition (usually mid-June, EventCity, Manchester)

Details of all of the above at:
www.franchiseinfo.co.uk/exhibitions-across-the-uk

The Franchise Show (usually mid-February, ExCeL, London)

www.thefranchiseshow.co.uk

Regional franchise shows (various dates across the UK)

Educational seminars

British Franchise Association franchise seminars (various dates across the UK)

www.thebfa.org

NatWest franchise seminars (various dates across the UK)

www.franchise-seminars.info

Focus points

* Make sure that you have decided your long-term goals at the outset.
* Your research shouldn't just be performed behind a computer screen – visit the head offices and speak to existing franchisees. Ask them the difficult questions.
* It is worth educating yourself about franchising as much as possible by attending educational seminars (and reading this book!).
* Show the franchisor that you have done your research at this stage.
* Remember, the franchise agreement is a partnership, not a one-sided agreement. Don't treat any part of the purchasing process as a job interview.

Next step

Now that you have had some feedback from experienced franchisors, we will look in more detail about how you should approach a franchisor.

8

How to approach a franchisor

In this chapter you will learn:

► *How to prepare for approaching a franchisor*
► *How to conduct the initial approach*
► *What to look out for in your initial conversations*
► *The things that you should be wary of at this stage.*

Once you have narrowed down your shortlist, you will need to start approaching franchisors. It is important to remember that the franchisor has invested a lot of time, effort and money in building its brand, so it wants to ensure that you will be the right partner to achieve mutual success. The franchisor will also not want to have a franchisee failure on its hands, as this will reflect badly in terms of a bank's view of its network. It will also have a significant drain on head office resources, since it will need to manage the situation pre-failure. Finally, the other franchisees will be affected by a fellow franchisee failing, and this will impact on the overall network morale.

You should prepare for this approach in the same way that you would prepare for a job interview: before you even pick up the phone, or email the franchisor, research the company and learn as much as you can about it. This advice might seem very basic; but it's surprising how many people enter the first stage of the communication process blindly. This preparation will put you in good stead for the development of the conversations, as most franchisors will look to filter their applicants during the initial contacts so that they only devote significant time to the ones that they consider are serious about investing in their network.

This is perhaps even more so nowadays, given that the Internet has allowed prospective franchisees to contact several franchisors at once, simply by selecting the ones that they wish to obtain more information from. Previously, prospective franchisees had to phone each and every franchisor, and spend far more time around the initial process during 'work' hours. Thanks to the Internet, there are more hours available overall and less time devoted to each initial contact – perhaps a recipe for drunken 2am enquiries to each and every franchisor in a particular directory!

Given the first paragraph, it goes without saying that all communications should be professional. Make sure that there are no spelling mistakes in your emails, and that you are communicating clearly. When meeting a franchisor, make sure that you are projecting the image that you wish to project, as though you were applying for a very senior job at their organization. There will be an element of the recruitment process that becomes 'salesy', but you do need to bear in mind that it is a two-way process at all times, and the franchisor will be cautious of any red flags that you may inadvertently raise during their discussions and communications with you.

Comments from franchisors

Rather than just providing my view on how to approach a franchisor, I've asked some well-known franchisors in the industry to provide their tips for approaching a franchisor:

'My advice would be to thoroughly research the company's website and use the contact details shown in the website. Usually, the first contact will be via email or the website contact form, therefore please use this as a positive opportunity to sell yourself and impress the franchisor.'

Ken Deary, Right at Home

'Don't discount a franchisor that appears to be "beneath you" – some of the best partnerships I've seen are those that have come from the corporate world and have selected a franchise that might appear to be blue collar. Sometimes, professionals prefer a white-collar franchise as it lies within their comfort zone; however, they might have a more profitable and more saleable franchise if they were to employ a "team of men in a team of vans", to adapt a well-known phrase!

When you have decided on a franchise to approach, make sure you pick up the phone and speak to the franchise director: it's important that you have a shared vision and that they are as ambitious and smart as you. You also need to know about the executive team's track record of dealing with problems – what issues have they had in the past, how did they deal with them, and, most importantly, are they being transparent with you about these.'

Simon Mills, Seriously FUN Swimming Schools

'Remember that in a well-established franchise brand, the franchisor actually has more at stake than you do. They need to ensure that you are a safe pair of hands in which to place their precious brand. You begin to project an impression of yourself

*every time you communicate with the franchisor, so a good way
to think about this is to view it as if you were applying for a
job at the franchisor's head office. If you send in poorly worded
or curt emails, they will assume that is how you will treat your
(and their) customers, and won't be impressed.*

*Similarly, if you turn up late for appointments, or fail to read
the directions they sent you and get lost on the way, then again
they will assume this is how you conduct yourself in general and
may think twice about taking you on. Too many franchisees
assume that they are the ones doing the franchisor a favour by
joining them, but in a successful, well-structured franchise it
really isn't the case! A good, ethical franchisor won't be giving
you the 'hard sell'; it will be continually assessing you to make
sure you are a good fit for its brand. If a franchisor concludes
that you aren't, don't be too upset by this. The franchisor will
probably know better than you what is being looked for and
may just have done you a favour.'*

Steve Felmingham, Banana Moon Day Nurseries

*'While prospects frequently treat a meeting like a job interview,
this is not a very healthy way to act. I don't have a job for you
that you can talk your way into and then leave if you don't
enjoy it. You are paying money for this. And we are investing
time and energy in you in return. The interview is actually a
TWO-WAY process.*

*Here's an example – if you don't like mornings and the 'job'
says you have to start at 8am every day, you might just be able
to carry it off without a problem. You'll probably survive in
the job for a while and be OK. But will you excel? Unlikely –
because you're squeezing a square peg into a round hole.*

*We expect our pegs to identify the shape of the hole, see where
they might not fit, check that it can be worked around and walk
away if the shapes don't match. We met a really charming man
and his wife at one interview. They lived in a place we knew
to be a good possibility for a thriving business. They were very
engaged in discussions and said "yes" to everything. On the
face of it a perfect match. I was surprised, but happy, when
the wife called me a few days in and said they weren't going to*

take it any further because they'd been kidding themselves – the husband couldn't use a screwdriver! His practical skills were a joke in the family. It was an honest moment that saved him a lot of struggle and challenge. It was the right decision. And we were delighted to introduce him to another franchisor that he eventually joined! Be honest about YOURSELF.'

Louise Harris, Wilkins Chimney Sweep

'Firstly, find a business that you feel passionate about: when running your own business the more passion and belief you have in the business the more successful you will make it. It's not just about financials – you have to enjoy what you do.

Have a thorough read through the franchise prospectus – does it give a full description of the opportunity? Clear set up costs? Financial predictions? Be prepared to answer a short application form. Any ethical franchisor has a responsibility to its current network to take on suitable franchisees.

Make sure there is an open day, discovery day or similar where you get to meet the franchisor. You will be working with this person/team for usually a minimum of five years so make sure you feel confident in them. Ask plenty of questions and be happy that all of them are answered confidently and openly.

Finally, be yourself; any franchisor will conduct an interview when they meet you so be open and honest – being a franchisee is a two-way street so as well as trusting them they must be able to trust you to give you the best support possible.'

Anne-Marie Martin, franchisor Diddi Dance

'When in the process of evaluating your franchise opportunity, make sure the franchisor gives you permission to speak to any franchisee in the network. Do not be steered by their preferences for you to speak to their top performing branches. While tempting, a good franchisor will be happy for you to speak to any franchisees at your request. Ensure plenty of time to undertake this important part of your due diligence. Try to speak to as many existing franchisees, understanding what business is like on a day-to-day basis and also how much cross-collaboration exists, etc. Ask how frequently the whole business meets, the style *of those meetings and franchisee engagement. Speak to a range of support staff across the franchisor's business. Your day-to-day engagement will be across this support team. Understand how franchisees grow their business and what effort they put into marketing. Check the systems and processes in place to help win and retain customers. Clarify with franchisees the most effective marketing channels and level of return you might expect.*

These following elements are critical in assessing franchise opportunities. Is the business fully accredited with the British Franchise Association (bfa)? This is a kitemark of quality for ethical franchisors who are frequently re-accredited against its standards. Through a code of ethics, the franchisor business must disclose a range of detail regarding its business. For example: a record of success and failure, who are the key people in the business, their background experience, etc. An ethical franchisor will have no problem sharing this information. Most bfa-accredited franchisors will insist you use a bfa solicitor to advise you on the purchase of the franchise. This is excellent practice ensuring guidance, but also a solicitor operating within the franchising community will already have an opinion on how the franchisor conducts its business.'

Mike Parker, franchisor Minster Cleaning Services

'The initial contact with the franchisor directly should be by phone to its offices, and ask to speak to the person who looks after franchise recruitment. The way the franchisor handles your initial enquiry will give you a big insight into how professional it is as a business. When you get through to the right person, listen intently to how he or she speaks. Is it in a proficient manner, are they confident in what they are saying?

During this initial call it is essential to ask searching questions such as: What is the success rate of the current franchisees? (Don't be afraid to ask how many failures they have had.) How long has the franchisor been trading? What is the franchisor's background? Who are the key people in the operation – directors, business managers? Who in the operation will support you as a franchisee and what are their backgrounds? What is the franchisor's target market and what is the demand like in your area? It may be that all the points you have found out during your research are confirmed; if this is not the case then do probe further to find out why the answers may differ. Don't forget to ask about the selection process as this will give you an idea of the credibility of the franchisor; be very wary of anyone who basically tells you that "if you have the money you can have a franchise" – what does this tell you about the business... does the franchisor really care about the network or is it in the business of making money from selling franchises rather than creating a network of successful and profitable franchisees?'

Dave Galvin, franchisor Dwyer Group (comprising Mr Electric, Aire Serv and Drain Doctor)

'If I could give one piece of advice to new franchisees about how to approach a franchisor, it would be that they should be well informed before making contact – in respect of franchising, the business that they are approaching, but also themselves: they need to make sure that starting a franchise is right for them.'

Rob Oyston, Sports Xtra

'The key to choosing a franchise revolves around several issues, including making sure that you select a franchisor that has a proven track record in franchising, a franchise model that shows some longevity and is not "fad" based. I would never seriously consider a franchise opportunity that did not carry the British Franchise Association kitemark. At the end of the day, after this process, you need to ensure that it's something that you are going to enjoy doing with a franchisor that you enjoy interacting with. I personally believe that it is always better to approach the potential franchisor with a phone call rather than a cold email, if possible. At this point you should have already done some research about the nature of the franchise, the franchisor, and also have in mind the sort of questions that you would wish to ask the franchisor.'

Laurence Bagley, Bardon Group (comprising Recognition Express, ComputerXplorers, The Zip Yard and Kall Kwik)

'I always looked for confidence and a good degree of preparation from franchisee prospects. Rightly or wrongly

the interview process starts from the initial contact, so first impressions really do matter. As a franchisor I made sure there was a lot of useful information about the company easily available for anyone interested. My advice to a prospective franchisee would be to make sure you do a reasonable level of research before getting in touch; a franchisor will be much more open and sharing with someone who has demonstrated they have a genuine interest in the franchise opportunity.

Some people march into franchisee Discovery Days determined to tell you what's wrong with your business model and how they have a far better way of doing it and are in fact weighing up their options to decide if they could do it better themselves. I'm stating the obvious here, but that's not going to get you off to a good start!

While I would advise taking a meeting with a franchisor as seriously as you would a normal job interview, I do think there is a more grown-up attitude to these things within franchising. Both sides should want to impress the other; however, there should also be a meeting of minds in terms of the way you both like to do business and the culture and environment that you both like to work within. Finding a natural and easy fit is likely to be the most important thing that both parties will be looking for initially. Be yourself, be relaxed, be friendly – a good franchisor will always welcome plenty of questions so always attend meetings armed with stacks of them.

The successful progression of the right franchisee in the right franchise is a beautiful sight to behold. Choose wisely, because I firmly believe that franchising offers the ambitious and hardworking individual with the single best opportunity to own their own business that there is.'

Suzie McCafferty, former franchisor and Managing Director of Platinum Wave

'Ensure the franchisor is a bfa member and that it gives you a full list of franchise owners to talk to about its model. For me, you must always visit the franchisor's premises, too, to get a feeling for the people and culture of the business. Are the staff

enthused, are they friendly, do you like them? It is so important that the culture matches you and your ambitions.

Be open, honest and friendly about what you want to achieve. Don't keep anything back, because if you do you are not being honest and this will not be good for what is a long-term investment and opportunity.'

Phil Harrison, Envirovent

'Preparation is key. Make sure you understand their recruitment process – what are they looking for, how long does it take and how many steps are there?

1 *Look at case studies of existing franchisees – do you fit these profiles? Are you a typical franchisee? Your personality needs to fit the industry and the company. Show that you're compatible and that you would be the perfect fit for the franchise network. Do you love animals, like working with people or enthusiastic about food? You'll need to demonstrate this through examples of previous work, achievements, your personality, life experience, hobbies, interests, passions, beliefs, etc.*

2 *Demonstrate that you're able to run that type of business. Are you cut out to manage a busy restaurant environment with 100-plus staff, or on the road dashing about to meet customers, or happy to sit at a desk for hours on end? Do you have the right skills to own this type of business? Don't worry if you haven't worked in that industry before. People gain invaluable skills such as being organized through life experience, e.g. juggling busy households or managing challenging commitments outside work.*

3 *Franchisors will want to know how you will be funding the startup costs and whether you have enough capital to live on and to invest in premises, stock, etc. Make sure you research funding options and have a plan in place for when the franchisor asks.*

4 *Come loaded with relevant questions. It shows you're serious about becoming a franchisee.*

5 *Most importantly show willing and be enthusiastic. Running a franchise is hard work and you need to have the guts and steely determination to make it a success.'*

Jo Tomlinson, franchisor We Love Pets

Focus points

- Make sure that you present the right image in all communications, from first email through to head office visit.
- Ask for details about any problems as well as the sales pitch! The important part is whether they acknowledge any previous problems in their network and, most importantly, how they dealt with them... no business is perfect!
- Always remember that the franchisor isn't just selling – it has its brand at stake and will be approaching you with caution until satisfied that you won't let it down.
- As mentioned in previous chapters, nothing beats talking and face-to-face conversations. Speak to both head office and existing franchisees.
- Make sure that the franchisor is a good 'fit' for you, and that you feel comfortable signing a long-term agreement.
- Be prepared – research, research, research!

Next step

This chapter is probably one of the most valuable chapters you will read in this book, because you have heard tips from the people on the other side of the table. In the next chapter we will put the focus on what you should be looking for in a franchise.

9

What you should look for in a franchise

In this chapter you will learn:

▶ *The questions that you should ask a franchisor*

▶ *The questions that a franchisor may ask you*

▶ *The support that you should be given.*

The franchise marriage

A key thing to remember when weighing up whether a franchise is right for you is that it is a long-term commitment, which I often refer to as the 'franchise marriage'. When you sign a franchise agreement, you are usually signing into a business relationship for five years (renewable), and over that time there will be ups and downs, just like in any marriage! Because of this, it's important that you are happy that the franchisor is the right partner in this agreement, and that you are comfortable with the arrangement and the way things are done.

You should weigh up whether the franchisor's values are aligned with yours, and whether you are happy with the levels of support from the head office team. Also, it's worth making sure that you have an aligned sense of purpose and vision for the overall brand. By making sure that you consider these items before signing the franchise agreement, it reduces the risk of things going wrong further down the line, and in turn both parties having to seek legal remedies to get any issues resolved.

It's also essential to make sure that it is the right type of business opportunity for you. You should bring together the questions raised in the previous chapters to ensure that the franchise will fulfil your expectations over the course of the agreement: How big is the territory? Is it an operational or management franchise? What is the scope for expansion? Is an area developer or master franchise agreement more appropriate for you?

Key idea: View from a franchise expert

There are more than 900 different business opportunities currently available and the number is growing year on year. There's a wide choice of franchises in a variety of business categories – fine dining restaurants, pizza delivery, domiciliary care, plumbing, cleaning ovens, gardening, property sales and letting, and many more. Those seeking a franchise can therefore usually find a business that suits.

It does, however, mean that choosing the right franchise can be a challenging exercise. Having worked in franchising for more than

25 years, managing several franchised businesses, including Dyno-Rod, Snack-in-the-Box and Ovenclean, I have met many people who are trying to find a suitable business opportunity. **My advice to them is, firstly, to be clear about the primary requirement.**

* Is it to bring about a change in work routine?
* Is it intended to provide a better work/life balance?
* Is it to improve long-term earnings and prosperity?
* Is it to simply feel that destiny is more controlled?
* Is it just because it seems like a good option?

Not surprisingly, the answer often touches on all of these issues, but to varying degrees. Identifying the most important requirements will, however, be key to refining the type of franchise that would be most suited. Or, even if buying a franchise is the best option at all!

The next question will revolve around the task of aligning the candidate's character and personality with the right type of business. Sometimes this can be difficult because it requires the candidate to be very honest about their strengths and weaknesses, but past experience and an appraisal of skills will invariably steer a course towards the type of business that should be focused on.

The following examples can help to illustrate.

Example 1

Background

John is a 45-year-old married man with two children. He has worked as a car mechanic for his entire career but has recently been made redundant and using his redundancy payment, plus savings, he would like to buy a franchise. He is a proud family man who is bright, hard-working and personable, but has limited commercial ability. He wants a franchise that would allow him to exploit his practical skills and to work on his own.

Type of franchise

A 'man and van' repair and maintenance franchise, perhaps in the automotive sector, e.g. smart repair. It is a franchise that is not dependent on selling ability but provides a flow of regular repeat business through the application of good interpersonal skills.

Example 2

Background

Martin is an accomplished sales manager of a printing company. He is 40 years old, married with a young daughter. He is money motivated and enjoys a good remuneration but is a frustrated employee. He is fed up of the usual work routine and has identified franchising as the way forward. He is outgoing and highly ambitious. He has plenty of equity in his house and financial assistance is available from his family.

Type of franchise

A medium-to-high investment management franchise requiring the building of a team in which professional sales skills would be a key to success. This might be a catering or retail business, possibly instant print.

It is not unusual for prospective franchise owners to seek an opportunity that is vastly different to the field of work they have been in. The requirement is a real lifestyle change. So, it might be possible that Martin would be attracted to the type of business that John pursues, and vice versa. But that obviously increases the risk.

There are 44,000 franchise owners in the UK, all with the chance to fulfil their ambition of being their own boss due to the brand and support the franchisor provides. They have varying personalities but there are common attributes they all share – drive, enthusiasm and a determination to succeed.

Clive Smith, franchisor MagicMan and franchise consultant at Franchise Intelligence

Questions you should ask

There is a range of questions that you should ask any franchisor before committing, and some of my suggested questions are as follows. I don't suggest that you reel off all of these, instead you should review the list to help you think about the types of question that you should ask:

1 How long have you been in business?

2 How long have you been actively franchising your business?

3   Did you run a company-owned pilot operation?

4   How many franchisees do you have operating?

5   How many franchisees do you take on per year?

6   How do you select your franchisees?

7   How many franchise failures have you had?

8   What are the reasons for any franchise failures?

9   Can you provide a complete list of franchise locations?

10   Can you provide any references?

11   Can you provide your (franchisor) financial statements?

12   Can you provide anonymized benchmarking information/ financial reports for your franchisees?

13   How have your projections been compiled? Are they based on a territory similar to mine?

14   Have you taken professional advice in respect of the compilation of projections?

15   Do you have arrangements with any of the high street banks?

16   Do you have any referees that I can speak to outside of the franchise network?

17   Are you a member of the British Franchise Association? If not, why not?

18   How much is the initial franchise fee?

19   What level of training is involved? What is the fee for this? Is there any supplementary training once I've got started?

20   How much is the working capital requirement over and above the initial franchise fee?

21   What is the ongoing management service fee?

22   Are there any other monthly obligations, such as a contribution to a central marketing fund?

23 How is the central marketing fund spent?

24 Are there any requirements to use centrally sourced suppliers?

25 Is there any review of these suppliers to ensure that they provide the network with a good service?

26 Do franchisees obtain a preferential rate from these suppliers?

27 Do you accept commissions from these suppliers?

28 What level of support can I expect from the head office team?

29 Which members of the head office team will I be dealing with on a day-to-day basis? How are they trained, and will they have the experience to support me with my business?

30 Can I meet my main contact at head office, if I haven't already?

31 How often can I expect contact from head office? How often can I expect a visit from a regional manager?

32 Will you perform a quality control audit on me, and if so how often? Is this the same across the network? If not, how can I be sure that a neighbouring franchisee isn't affecting the brand?

33 Do you have any mentoring available to new franchisees? Can I spend time with existing franchisees to learn the ropes?

34 How often do franchisees meet at conferences or regional forums? Is there a cost attached to these?

35 How do you provide the operations manual? Has it been prepared by you or by a professional?

36 What support do you provide me with in relation to promoting the franchise locally?

37 Do you provide a centralized website or social media presence?

38 What support do you provide should I wish to develop my business beyond my initial projections?

39 What happens if I get a customer from outside of my territory? Am I able to purchase a second territory should I maximize the potential of my first?

40 What happens if I don't meet my projected targets in my business plan?

41 How will you help ensure that I meet my business plan?

42 What happens if I don't reach my minimum performance targets?

43 Can I see a copy of the agreement between us?

44 Has the agreement been prepared by a bfa-affiliated solicitor?

45 Am I allowed to sell my franchise?

46 Are there any restrictions on who I can sell my franchise to?

47 How long is the agreement for?

48 Is there an option for renewal at the end of the franchise term?

49 Are there any key restrictions that I should be aware of?

50 What happens if I decide that the franchise is not for me during the agreement?

The above list of questions is by no means comprehensive, and you might think of lots of others that are more specific to the business that you are looking at. The important thing is to ensure that you ask a range of questions about all areas of the franchise – starting with the buying process, right the way through to the end of the agreement; and covering various eventualities (both good and bad) in the interim.

Remember this: Advice from a franchisor

Prospective franchisees must feel comfortable asking 'awkward' questions. For example, ensure you ask about previous failures that the franchisor has had in the network. Understand why and establish whether these reasons were down to the franchisee or lack of support, training, etc. on the part of the franchisor. Discuss the franchise agreement renewal situation. A discussion with your solicitor early on should establish the franchisor's procedure. For instance, we allow ongoing automatic renewals without limit. Others will limit the number of renewals and others will not permit renewal without further payment.

Ask the franchisor about their income streams. Businesses like ours make their money directly from the turnover of franchisees. Ask about other compulsory purchases such as materials, add-on benefits and services, which in some cases have to be purchased through the franchisor's designated suppliers. If this is the case, establish what the franchisor makes – this should be transparent.

Establish whether the business you're investing in is a real business, in that when you come to retire or leave, there's a business to sell. This can be discovered quickly by asking the franchisor for examples of existing businesses for sale to see exactly what is available. Understanding the valuation metrics that impact on sales value will help you focus on building a valuable business for when you retire.

Mike Parker, franchisor Minster Cleaning Services

Questions a franchisor should ask

As you should understand by now, the franchise recruitment process is a two-way process, and you should expect the franchisor to ask you a range of questions as well. It is much harder to define these as most franchisors will have particular requirements in respect of their network; however, you can broadly be expected to answer the following questions, along with many more, at some point in the process:

1 Have you had any experience running a franchise before?

2 Have you had any experience in this industry before?

3   Why have you chosen this particular sector?

4   Why have you chosen to invest in a franchise rather than start a new business yourself?

5   What are you looking to get from the franchise relationship?

6   How long and how hard are you willing to work to make this a success?

7   What skills do you have that you can bring to the table to build the franchise?

8   What is your background in sales and business development?

9   Why have you chosen us as your potential franchisor?

10 How will you finance the franchise?

11 Are you prepared for the possibility of not meeting your projections? What is your contingency plan?

12 Do you have support from your partner and your family? Do you have another form of income in your household?

13 Why do you feel that you would be a good fit for our network?

14 What is your exit strategy?

Remember this: Advice from a franchisor

While you're evaluating the business you're considering investing in, equally the franchisor should be taking time to assess you as a prospective franchisee. **If you feel the franchisor is not interested in your skillset and suitability, be very careful**. For us, long-term relationships are important and we are selective about who we bring into our business. We are not interested in turning our franchisees over regularly to acquire repeat fees, because as with any ethical franchisor we align our fee income (management service fee) to the underlying trade of the franchisee.

Mike Parker, franchisor Minster Cleaning Services

Ongoing support

Perhaps the main area that you should investigate when asking questions of the franchisor is the ongoing support provided. Many franchises have a slick sales process, and teams of franchise recruiters who can persuade you to sign the agreement. You are, however, buying into a very long term business agreement, and as such you need to make sure that the obligations are shared on both sides.

Typically, you would expect a new franchise to be managed by the founder; however, as the network grows you should expect that person to be supported by a franchise management team at head office. The point at which a franchisor needs to appoint a support team varies, based on the level of support that they provide, and also whether they are still running company-owned operations. I would, however, expect most franchises to have employed a dedicated franchise professional by the time that they have reached 20 franchisees, as this tends to be the point where it is too much for the founder to manage alone.

Key idea: Advice from an expert

One of the main advantages of investing in a franchise is the training and support provided by the franchisor. This should equip franchisees to deliver the actual service or product, often in an industry new to them, and equally important, help them to manage and grow a successful business. Like all industries, there are some franchisors who provide fantastic support but others where this is more limited. So what should you look for in a franchise?

Initial training and support

When becoming a franchisee, there are two types of initial training that you should expect to receive:

Technical training

Many franchisees have no previous experience in the sector and some franchisors actually prefer this – it means they are easier to mould and won't have picked up any bad habits. The technical training should equip franchisees to deliver the actual service or product and will focus on operational processes. For example, for a gardening franchise this may include training on how to use the equipment and administer lawn pesticides.

Business training

Many franchisees have not run their own business before. The franchisor's training should cover all the key aspects designed to help franchisees manage and grow a successful business. This could include sales and marketing training, advice on recruiting staff and understanding management accounts. Comprehensive business training often sets the best franchisors apart.

Ongoing support

Once a franchisee has established his or her business, ongoing support should help grow this and build a business asset that can be sold some day. Look for three levels of ongoing support:

Head office support

For most franchises, there will be several head office departments, like marketing, which are focused on helping them grow their customer base: IT that provides and maintains key systems; HR that provides advice on recruiting and staying compliant with the latest employment regulations, and so on.

Face-to-face support

Franchisees are often assigned a franchise support manager – they meet with franchisees on a one-to-one basis at regular intervals to review their business plans, discuss key challenges and coach them to grow their businesses.

Peer support

Since other franchisees are walking the same path, they can provide a valuable support network. Good franchisors cultivate a community of franchisee-to-franchisee best practice sharing through regional meetings, an annual conference and/or online portal.

Checklist

When evaluating the initial training and support provided by a franchisor, look at the specifics:

▶ **What initial training is provided?** Is this delivered by the franchisor or is it outsourced?

▶ **How will the franchisor help you to recruit your first customers?**

▶ **How big is the head office team** and what is the ratio between support staff and franchisees?

▶ As the number of franchisees grows, **does the franchisor plan on growing the head office team** so that this support isn't diluted?

▶ **How often will you meet on a face-to-face basis** with a franchise support manager?

▶ **Speak with existing franchisees** – would they recommend the franchisor? How do they rate the training and support?

Steven Frost, Director, Smith & Henderson

Hopefully, you will now have a much greater understanding of what you should be asking of your franchisor, and what your franchisor should be asking of you. The franchisee recruitment process really is a two-way thing, and you should be reassured by the above comments from franchisors that they want you to ask the difficult questions. Every franchisor is looking for their franchisees to be commercially savvy, and by being prepared for the franchisee recruitment process you can demonstrate this.

Focus points

✻ The 'franchise marriage' is longer than many real marriages, and it can sometimes be just as difficult to divorce. Make sure that you choose the right partner!

✻ Go into the conversations with your franchisor with a range of questions about him or her and the franchise.

✻ Don't be afraid to deviate from the suggested list of questions. You might find that your conversations naturally lead you to unexpected questions – the key is that you ask the right questions to give you the comfort that you are investing in the right franchise.

✻ Sometimes, the more uncomfortable the question the better it is. Franchisors want to see that you are going to be commercially aware.

* While it is hard to define a list of questions that a franchisor may ask you, there are some key questions that you should be prepared for.
* A good proportion of what you are paying for through your Management Service Fees is head office support – make sure you know what you are getting.

Next step

Having satisfied yourself that you understand what your chosen franchise has to offer, your next move is to carry out due diligence checks and heed five major warning signs.

Checks that you should perform before committing and the five warning signs

In this chapter you will learn:

▶ *Why you should look for bfa member franchises*

▶ *What steps you can take to ensure a franchise offering is what you are expecting*

▶ *Five warning signs that you must be aware of.*

the shortlist to the network that you with, you should now perform due nat your investment is safe. There are simple take to make sure that you are investing in rtunity. These steps might lead you to having to n all over again; however, this is a far preferable e alternative of investing in a network that doesn't basic checks.

bfa accreditation and the Code of Ethics

One of the simplest checks that you can do is to see whether your prospective franchisor is a member of the British Franchise Association. Every member of the bfa has been through a rigorous accreditation procedure, which helps reassure the public that the business model is both proven and set up correctly.

Key idea: Advice from the bfa

Ethical franchising is the fundamental cornerstone of the British Franchise Association and it is through our standards-based accreditation process that member franchisors differentiate themselves as following good franchising practice.

The bfa has a set of rules of membership and a Code of Ethics against which we hold our members.

The Code of Ethics originates from the European Franchise Federation and, as intended, has been adapted for the UK market. Franchisors must satisfy strict criteria in order to become bfa members – each year, companies that cannot meet our standards are refused membership.

What do we look at as part of the accreditation process? Broadly speaking:

* **Legal agreement** – the franchise agreement is an important document that governs the relationship between the franchisor and franchisee for the duration of the franchise. The bfa reviews the agreement to ensure that it meets the standards and minimum terms associated with ethical franchising.

* **Financial information** – the financial stability of the franchisor is important so that we know they have the funds to support a growing franchisee network. The financial projections given to franchisees are also reviewed and assessed and there is a requirement that they are appropriately disclosed and disclaimed: we require documented proof that what is being 'promised' to prospective franchisees has been achieved, by either the pilot model or other franchisees in the network.
* **Marketing and advertising** – the material is regularly reviewed to ensure that it does not misrepresent information, such as false financial claims or over-promises.
* **Operations manual** – this is assessed to ensure that it has the relevant information to assist a new franchisee.
* **Training and support** – these are evaluated and must be substantive enough to launch and sustain new franchisees.

If there are franchisees in the network we conduct a confidential survey to ask them about the franchisor, specifically regarding the support offered and financial projections given – and whether they are realistic. In this way franchisees can inform the bfa, confidentially, of any concerns.

It is only when franchisors have provided all of the necessary information and demonstrated how they meet the standards that they can attain bfa membership status. Through this process the bfa helps prospective franchisees recognize good franchisors in the marketplace. Although membership is **not a guarantee of success**, it is recognition that we have evaluated the franchise model and the company's interactions with its franchisees – a significant sign that prospective franchisees should look for.

Kelly Chambers-Lee, Head of Compliance, the British Franchise Association

Due diligence

While due diligence might not seem to be the most exciting part of investing in a franchise, it is a necessary function to avoid a potentially very expensive mistake! Checking bfa membership, as mentioned above, is just one part of this.

I regularly speak to prospective franchisees about what to look for when investing in a franchise, and perhaps the most important piece of due diligence work that you can do is to talk to existing franchisees. Any franchisor should provide you with a full list of franchisees to contact, and this list shouldn't just be edited to include the happy ones! Having said that, it is worth speaking to the franchisor to see if there are any franchisees that are particularly recommended for you to speak to, as there may be franchisees who have similar experience levels as you, or are operating under similar conditions. Be sure to ask the franchisees that you speak to if they are happy with the network, and ultimately if they would recommend that you join the network.

Desk research on the Internet is another possibility, but approach this with caution – remember that most reviews posted online are either negative or fake! It is rare that the happy purchasers of any service or product proactively take to reviewing their experience online; while those with problems (or competitors) are more than happy to share their experiences, real or fake.

Remember this: Advice from a franchisor

Making the journey away from employment and working for yourself is a big decision in anyone's life. There are a number of avenues that can be taken to reach your goals, franchising being just one. My whole career has been in franchising, from being a successful franchisee for more than 18 years to working with franchisors developing their networks. **It is an amazing avenue to personal and financial achievement but one sadly that people often do not enter with their eyes open, and set themselves up for failure that can so easily have been avoided.**

I have watched so many candidates listen to sales pitches, read the words from the pages of the franchisors' brochures and allowed their dreams to move them forward to sign their franchise agreements. I would liken this behaviour to someone getting married who only focuses on the big day and not on their lives ahead. The dating has gone well and the candidate likes the franchisor and the franchisor likes the candidate; you have probably met some of the family:

✱ The franchisor has shared its business model, met the candidate's spouse and completed the background checks

✳ The candidate understands the business model, has met the majority of the franchisor's team and has spoken to some of the franchisees.

Due diligence complete? Pen ready?

I want you to stop for a moment...

Have you ever booked a package holiday after poring over a holiday brochure? You read the description over and over, you book, you read the description again, you save up, purchase lots of nice new clothes, you read the description again and off you go. The plane lands... you know it's a short ride since the brochure said so... excited? You're almost there... 5-minute ride... just like the brochure said. Happy? The coach stops and there is your hotel... on the flight path and the pool is at the end of the runway! It's not what you thought is it? But the description did say 'close to the airport' but you thought great, no long coach ride!

What could you have done differently? DUE DILIGENCE.

When you called the franchisees: What did you ask? What did they tell you? Did the franchisor give you a complete list of ALL its franchisees or did it supply its 'A' list? Did you ask the questions that would have given you the true understanding you needed to decide to go into this business? Due diligence is NOT what the franchisor wants you to know or tell you.

A candidate who wishes to become a successful franchisee needs to complete due diligence that includes the pitfalls, failures and what is required of them to run the business successfully. This is valuable information and will allow you to work productively with your franchisor to enable joint success.

Bev Regan, franchisor Aspect and former franchisee

Financial due diligence is another area that is important to go through. While the franchisor might offer you projections and demonstrate the performance of existing franchisees, you should seek professional advice to ensure that the projections stack up, and are appropriate for your territory and projected scale of operations. For example, you might be provided with historic accounts for a franchisee in a small town where the rents are far lower than the national average, let alone a property in London or Edinburgh.

Finally, remember not to limit your financial due diligence to the projections that you are provided with. Be sure to review the franchisors' financial statements to ensure that they are suitably capitalized, and are likely to be in business for the duration of the franchise agreement!

Key idea: Advice from a legal expert

Not all franchises are equal and the reality may fall very short of what was promised at the outset. **Due diligence and investigation before signing a franchise agreement can help avoid nasty surprises later.**

Obtaining a review of the franchise agreement from a solicitor experienced in franchising should form part of any due diligence process, regardless of whether the franchise agreement has been issued as a non-negotiable document or whether the franchisor is an existing member of the British Franchise Association (bfa). The bfa has a list of approved affiliated solicitors who should be able to advise on how standard the agreement is, whether it conforms to the bfa's Code of Ethics and whether there are any glaring omissions or unusual provisions that may require investigation. **Although most franchise agreements are, by necessity, one sided in favour of the franchisor in order to protect the trade secrets and ensure quality control, there are checks and balances on the franchisor's powers, which should also be included.** The agreement can also be a good indicator of the franchisor's commitment to franchising and its success. A well-drafted agreement, prepared by an experienced law firm is not an insignificant investment by a franchisor and if a bfa-accredited franchise consultant has been engaged to advise on the operational aspects, even better.

Increasingly, franchisors who operate a successful core business will establish a new company to franchise out the business concept. This helps ring-fence liability and protect the core business if the franchised business fails. Therefore, the franchisor's corporate structure should be investigated to establish who owns the relevant intellectual property rights, that these rights have been correctly licensed to the franchisor entity and the financial solvency of the core business. The franchisor should be prepared to provide its marketing plan together with its latest set of accounts (and the previous three years if available). An accountant, experienced in franchising, should be engaged to review and advise on the financial projections provided by the franchisor, which should be based on fact not fiction, as well as the solvency of the franchisor itself.

The franchisor should confirm how many franchise agreements have terminated over the previous three years and the reasons for this. A high churn rate should prompt closer investigation and a breakdown of the initial franchise fee should be requested. **A franchisor should make its money from its ongoing management fee not from selling franchises. Be wary of any sharp marketing tactics adopted to induce a quick signing.**

Finally, and perhaps most importantly, **speak to as many of the existing franchisees as possible to establish what issues, if any, they have encountered in their franchised businesses and how these have been dealt with by the franchisor.** In order to avoid bias the franchisor should provide a full list of its franchisees, not just a cherry-picked few.

How a franchisor handles queries raised during the due diligence process can provide a good indication of what the future working relationship will be like. If a franchisor is not responsive and courteous at the outset it is unlikely to demonstrate these traits once the agreement is signed.

Nicola Broadhurst, partner/Head of Franchising, Stevens & Bolton

The five warning signs

While the previous chapters have given you some things to look for, both positive and negative, there are five major warning signs that you should look for in any network that you are talking to. If you see one of these, proceed with caution!

SALES VS RECRUITMENT

Perhaps one of the biggest warnings should come from a franchisor that is solely focused on selling to a prospective franchisee, as opposed to recruiting a potential franchisee. Now, I'm a realist, and am not of the view that the franchise recruitment process should be solely recruitment with no element of sales – the fact is that at least some sales process is required, otherwise the franchisor won't recruit any franchisee! But, it is important that the recruitment is a two-way process, and not simply a sales exercise.

To be able to spot this warning sign, you need to appreciate the difference between a sales approach and a recruitment approach. Generally, a sales approach would hide the potential problems that you might have in either your proposed territory or previous experience, and will be peppered with implied promises. Conversely, a recruitment approach would be more akin to a job interview, with no financial incentive. The franchisor would evaluate whether you are suitable for the opportunity, and actively look to turn away candidates who are not suitable for the franchise.

From a franchise network sustainability perspective, you should look for networks that take a 'recruitment' approach. Or, perhaps more importantly, proceed with caution if you are speaking to networks that focus on selling the opportunity and the dream!

FRANCHISEE CHURN

The next area that you need to look at is 'franchisee churn'. In plain English, what you want to know is how many franchisees have left the network.

Your franchisor should provide you with this information during your due diligence checks, and you should not only look at the number of franchisees leaving, but also the reasons why they have left the network. Depending on the maturity of the franchise network, there can be some valid reasons such as franchisee retirement, or preferably franchisee resale to a new incoming franchisee. The warning signs are what we would consider 'non-voluntary' reasons for leaving – mainly financial failure. If you see a trend of these, it would be worth having a frank conversation with the franchisor and, perhaps more importantly, interrogate the financial projections with the help of a professional adviser to ensure that you are entering into the franchise with your eyes open.

UNHAPPY FRANCHISEES

We discussed due diligence above, and one of the key checks that you should perform is informal conversations with existing franchisees. If these franchisees are unhappy or, worse, hidden from you by the franchisee, you need to proceed very carefully.

Bear in mind that each network will have a range of franchisees – the keen advocates, the unhappy few, and the majority who are in the middle. If your first couple of calls happen to be to unhappy franchisees, be sure to extend this process to widen the range of people who you are speaking to. If the message that you get continues to be negative, this will indicate a worrying trend that is likely to follow onto new franchisees as well as old!

UNDUE LIMITS AND EXPECTATIONS

While you should expect there to be restrictions within a franchise agreement, such as working within a defined territory, you should make sure that these restrictions and obligations are reasonable. For most people, it is difficult to identify the differences between reasonable and unreasonable restrictions, so this is an area where an independent legal review can pay for itself several times over.

One area that you should look at is whether your franchise territory is sufficient for you to generate the projected income. Make sure that you weigh up the demographics and population of the area that you are allocated to ensure that the income projections are reasonable. You should also review any minimum performance criteria that the franchisor has put in the franchise agreement. While a bfa member franchise has this reviewed as part of its accreditation, a non-member franchise is free to set any minimum performance criteria that it wishes without any reference to the actual performance of existing franchisees, and these may be overly onerous.

NEGOTIATIONS

Negotiations might seem like a good thing for you on the face of it. The franchisor might offer to reduce your initial investment, haggle a bit over the ongoing management service fee, and waive whatever clauses you want within the franchise agreement. While this might be superficially beneficial, it actually points towards a weak franchisor and/or a weak franchise system.

Any franchisor that is worth investing in should be clear that its franchise proposition is of value to you, and in turn is structured with an appropriate financial and operational structure to ensure a true 'win-win' partnership. An attempt to deviate from the initial proposition should sound alarm bells, since the franchisor is either desperate to shift 'units' by selling territories, or alternatively knows that the initial offering is unfair. Either situation is not ideal for the stability of the network as a whole.

Focus points

* If a franchisor is a bfa member, you know that an external standards-based trade association has reviewed its business.
* Importantly, bfa membership does not remove the responsibility on you to conduct full due diligence.
* If something appears to be too good to be true, it probably is.
* If you come across an overt sales pitch, high franchisee churn, too many unhappy franchisees, undue limits, or a franchisor who looks to negotiate fundamental terms – walk away.

Next step

In this chapter we've covered the areas of due diligence that you should perform. The warning signs are things to bear in mind, which hopefully will not arise during your purchase. In the next chapter we will learn more about the franchise agreement with the help of some legal experts.

Part Four

Purchasing the franchise

11

The franchise agreement

In this chapter you will learn:

- ▶ *The things that are covered in the franchise agreements*
- ▶ *Why you should take independent legal advice*
- ▶ *What you should look out for*
- ▶ *Some franchise-specific legislation.*

The franchise agreement underpins the relationship between franchisee and franchisor, and is effectively the summary of what both sides are bringing to the table in the business arrangement. While they are often weighty documents, it is important that you understand both the need for the franchise agreement, and what to look out for within the agreement.

As this is such an important legal document, I've asked a panel of expert franchising legal advisers to provide you with some advice to ensure that you don't make an expensive mistake.

Key idea: Advice from an expert

While the franchise relationship is often referred to as close, collaborative or a partnership, ultimately it is a legal relationship that is governed by the franchise agreement and other documents such as the operations manual. **Franchise agreements are by their nature complex. They are drafted by the franchisor's legal team to protect the franchisor.** The franchisor is, of course, providing franchisees with the franchisor's brand and its know-how.

Both of these elements are valuable and so a franchisor is justified in ensuring, through the provisions of the franchise agreement, that franchisees do not do anything that would harm or reduce the value of the brand and know-how. This is not only for the franchisor's protection but is also for the protection of other franchisees.

Most franchise agreements are 30 to 50 pages long and some are much longer. Just because the agreement is short does not mean that is a good thing. While it is easier to read short franchise agreements, they may not provide the level of protection for the franchisor and its network of franchisees.

The franchise agreement will set out in considerable detail exactly what it is that the franchisor and franchisees must do. Most of the obligations will be on the franchisee but there should also be obligations that are sufficiently precise to be enforceable on the franchisor.

The most important provisions for franchisees are:

Term – Most franchise agreements last for five years.

Renewal – If you are granted a five-year term you would expect the right to two automatic and no-cost renewals – one automatic renewal if your initial term is for ten years.

Territory – Virtually all franchise agreements contain a territory and they are not necessarily all exclusive.

Fees – First there is the *initial fee*, which should not contain a substantial profit element for the franchisor. Then there are *continuing fees*, usually calculated as a percentage of your turnover – commonly 8 per cent and, in addition, a *marketing fee* – usually 2 per cent. Ideally, there would not be any additional fees because the fee structure should be as simple as possible.

Mostly, franchisors refuse to amend their agreement because it becomes too time-consuming and expensive to negotiate every franchise agreement and would create all sorts of administrative headaches for a franchisor.

John Pratt, Hamilton Pratt

The need for independent legal advice

Perhaps the most commonly asked question that I receive from prospective franchisees, with regards to the legal agreement, is whether they have to obtain independent legal advice. My answer is always 'absolutely' – and then I usually enter into a long discussion about why you should use a solicitor who understands franchising, rather than a general commercial or family solicitor. In my opinion, there are two main reasons to use an expert:

▶ **Cost:** surprisingly, using an expert often ends up far cheaper than using a general practitioner. The reason for this is that most solicitors want to show value for their fees, and hence create a long list of potential issues and areas for negotiation. Realistically, as a franchisee you will not be able to get a franchisor to amend its terms, and it is also intended to be in the franchisor's favour in many areas! Therefore this negotiation becomes a waste of your money, and might lead you to not take on an agreement that is actually pretty normal for a franchise agreement. Franchise specialist advisers understand this, and hence look to protect you in respect of clauses that might be out of the ordinary when compared to other franchise agreements.

▶ **Industry knowledge:** an adviser who is established in franchising will be aware of who's who in the industry, the concepts that are successful, and ultimately will be able to advise you practically in respect of both the agreement and what to expect when you take on the franchise. This experience is invaluable, and simply not available from the vast majority of high street firms.

Now that we know why an expert should be used, it is worthwhile stepping back and understanding the general need for advice. Simply put, the agreement is a major commitment, which ties you in for a number of years and will require major financial input. Failing to perform simple checks on what you are purchasing (much as with the practical due diligence described above) can lead you to make a very expensive mistake – certainly, I'd hope most wouldn't purchase a house without a survey.

Key idea: Advice from an expert

Picture the scene... your meeting last week with the franchise manager of a franchise network you are interested in joining went really well. You were given plenty of information about the business and the fees you would be required to pay were clearly explained to you. You've just paid over a deposit and have reserved your territory. The franchisor has now sent you a franchise agreement and tells you to seek independent legal advice – what do you do?

(a) put the agreement in a drawer until you are ready to sign it – well, you understand the commercial terms and plenty of other franchisees have already signed the agreement;

(b) read the agreement carefully yourself and then sign it; or

(c) obtain legal advice on the terms of the agreement.

If you've answered (a) or (b), then think again. The correct answer is (c) every time. **Always ask a lawyer to review the franchise agreement before signing it.** The agreement is the document that will allow you to operate your business for many years to come; into which you have invested thousands of pounds. You may have also borrowed money from a bank and put your house on the line. **Don't start your business from a position of ignorance – make sure you fully understand its terms.**

Who should I ask to help?

You should ensure that any lawyer you use to review the franchise agreement is a specialist franchise lawyer who understands the franchising sector, understands how franchises operate and is familiar with the issues covered by a franchise agreement. It is highly recommended to use a law firm that is registered as an Affiliate of the British Franchise Association, as it has a proven track record of advising clients in the sector and all support ethical franchising.

What will a lawyer do for me?

In almost all instances a lawyer will prepare a report on the agreement, explaining its key terms, pointing out any provisions in the agreement that are unusually onerous and highlighting questions that you might want to raise with the franchisor.

A lawyer should also ensure that the trademark you are licensing has been registered. **A lawyer who is familiar with the sector will also be able to give you an indication of whether the franchise you are joining is reputable and whether the franchise agreement is well drafted** – indicating whether the franchisor has invested time, effort and money in putting in place a professional, well-drafted agreement.

Will the advice be expensive?

You should expect to pay legal fees in the hundreds of pounds for the preparation of a report on the franchise agreement.

Can I ask the franchisor to amend the franchise agreement?

Generally, the franchisor will not agree to any changes to the franchise agreement, especially if it is an established network. Franchisees, by and large, will all be subject to the same agreement. If, following discussions with the franchisor, a few minor changes to the franchise agreement are allowed, then these will normally be set out in a separate document to the main agreement.

Damian Humphrey, Ashton KCJ

Things to look out for

Key idea: Advice from an expert

It is important to know what should be included in a well-drafted franchise agreement, for example:

1. **The term of the agreement** – usually for a fixed term of five years but should be long enough for the franchisee to recoup his or her investment and make a profit.

2. **The conditions for renewal** should be clearly set out in the agreement and should not be prohibitive – no further initial fee should be payable.

3. **The territory granted to the franchisee** – exclusive or non-exclusive? If exclusive the minimum performance targets are acceptable if they are realistic and the franchisor acts ethically in their enforcement by giving the franchisee an opportunity to remedy any default.

4. **The obligations on the franchisor** – often quite short and written quite vaguely.

5. **The obligations on the franchisee** – usually lengthy and precise. They should set out what the franchisee must and must not do when operating the franchised business and all important obligations should be set out in the agreement and not left to the operating manual.

6. **The provisions relating to fees** – the initial fee should not be aimed at achieving a profit for the franchisor but should cover the initial costs and expenses in providing training and in the recruitment and launch of that franchisee. Any profit element for the franchisor should be confined to the continuing fees, the level of which should depend upon the success of the business – usually calculated as a percentage of the turnover of the franchisee.

7. Any **marketing levy** should be paid into a separate account and only be used to market the brand.

8. The franchise agreement should always contain **a right for the franchisee to sell** his or her business and should contain all of the conditions that must be met before consent to sale will be given. The franchisor usually charges a transfer fee but this should be no more than to cover costs and training.

9   The position in **the event of the death or incapacity of the franchisee**. The personal representatives of the franchisee should be able to realize the investment for the benefit of the estate by being able to transfer the business to a beneficiary or to an approved third party.

10 **The events which will allow for the immediate termination by the franchisor** should be clearly set out and listed in the agreement. These should be breaches that are incapable of remedy, such as non-payment of fees following a demand, ceasing to trade, insolvency, etc. The franchisee should be given a reasonable period of time in which to remedy any other breach as long as it is capable of remedy. The consequences of termination should also be listed clearly, stating what the franchisee must do at termination, for example returning the manual and confidential information.

11 The agreement will also include **restrictions on competition** that will apply during the term and after termination of the agreement. Following termination of the agreement, restrictions on competition are notoriously difficult to enforce and will only be upheld if they are no wider than is reasonably necessary to protect the franchisor's legitimate business interests. Generally, the restrictions should last no longer than one year and should be limited to competing activities within the areas in which the franchisee operated and where other franchisees operate.

12 The trademarks used in the system must be owned or licensed for use to the franchisor and the agreement should clearly state the position in relation to ownership and registration.

Nina Moran-Watson, NMW Legal/Franchise Consultancy Services

Why is 'xyz' in there?

Most of the contents of a franchise agreement are fairly standard, and to be expected in a general commercial agreement. There is, however, one area that I often get asked for advice on, where the incoming franchisee is expecting sales in the first year to be below the VAT registration threshold.

Usually, a franchise agreement contains an obligation for the franchisee to be VAT registered. This is sometimes incorrectly presumed by franchisees to be a mistake: in fact, it is required due to the Trading Schemes Act 1996.

Key idea: Advice from an expert

Franchise agreements often contain an obligation on a franchisee to register the business for VAT and remain registered throughout the duration of the franchise agreement. Some agreements go as far as making any failure to comply with this clause an issue that allows the franchisor to terminate the franchise agreement. But why do franchisors force franchisees (whose turnover is beneath the registration threshold) to register their business for VAT?

The Trading Schemes Act 1996

Put simply, the answer is to avoid the application of the Trading Schemes Act 1996 to the franchise system. This Act has often been considered the thorn in the side of ethical businesses that are hoping to expand via franchising. It was brought in to regulate the problems associated with 'pyramid selling'. The problem being that the 'franchisees' of a pyramid scheme are either directly encouraged to (or discover on their own) that it is more remunerative for them to find other sub-franchisees than to sell the goods or services that they are supposed to. In turn, these new recruits or 'sub-franchisees' are also told (or figure out) that they can make more money by recruiting their own 'sub-sub-franchisees'. This forms a pyramid like this:

Franchisor				*			
'Franchisee'			*	*	*		
'Sub-franchisee'		*	*	*	*	*	
'Sub-sub-franchisee'	*	*	*	*	*	*	*

These relationships are not illegal but they are heavily regulated by the Trading Schemes Act and the associated Trading Scheme Regulations 1997.

What's the problem for franchisors?

The problem is that the Act is very broad and generally all franchise relationships will be regarded as trading schemes under the Act (with limited exceptions). If the franchisor doesn't comply with the provisions of the Act they may face criminal prosecution. As such, any trading scheme must follow the Trading Scheme Regulations 1997 to the letter. These regulations are onerous and, in particular, impose tight controls relating to advertising, contractual provisions and cooling-off periods, which are unattractive to most franchisors.

So why do I have to be VAT registered?

There are two main exceptions to the Trading Schemes Act that enable the franchisor to avoid the regulations mentioned above. These are:

The franchise operates only on a **single tier**. For example:

Franchisor			*					
Franchisees	*	*	*	*	*	*	*	

OR

All UK-based franchisees are, and remain, registered for VAT. For example:

VAT-registered franchisor					*			
VAT-registered franchisee					*	*	*	
VAT-registered sub-franchisee			*	*	*	*	*	
VAT-registered sub-sub-franchisee	*	*	*	*	*	*	*	

With this in mind, it is clear why the franchisor requires VAT registration. However, if the franchisor is only operating on a single tier (as in the first exception above) then VAT registration may not be required. Often, franchisors will attempt to apply both exceptions in order to make sure there is no possibility that the franchise operation falls fouls of these regulations. They do this by prohibiting franchisees from taking on any self-employed individuals in the operation of the franchise business, as a self-employed individual may be deemed to constitute a 'second tier'.

Andrew Fraser, Harper Macleod

Focus points

* Generally, you should expect franchise agreements to be complex and one-sided. After all, they have been prepared at the franchisor's cost to protect the franchisor.

* Having said that, there are protections that you should expect within the agreement.

* You wouldn't buy a house without a survey, and by the same logic you shouldn't invest several thousand pounds in a franchise without an independent review of the agreement.

* Often, and perhaps counterintuitively, engaging a franchise specialist to perform an agreement review is cheaper since he or she won't look to argue matters that won't be changed.

* While franchising is unregulated, there is legislation, such as the Trading Schemes Act, which directly affects franchises. Most high street law firms would be unaware of the full implications of the Act.

Next step

In this chapter we've gained an understanding of the franchise agreement – particularly what should be included and why some unexpected obligations might have been put into the agreement. Next, we will look at the business plan.

12

The business plan

In this chapter you will learn:

▶ *Why you need to prepare a business plan*
▶ *What should be included in a business plan*
▶ *Where you can get advice on preparing a business plan*
▶ *What a franchisor looks for in a business plan.*

Preparing a business plan is probably one of the most time consuming yet important tasks during the purchasing process. Although many feel that it is simply used to obtain bank financing, the business plan is an excellent tool to help you appraise the franchise, understand the market that you will be entering into, and decide whether the franchise is the right one for you after considering all areas of the business and your competition.

This is a very important point that most prospective franchisees miss in their excitement to start the business. During the purchasing process I often see that decisions are made emotionally and, with the excitement of the new business prospect, many franchisees tend to be overly optimistic about the suitability of the franchise and its chances of succeeding. Going through the preparation of the business plan allows you to appraise the business honestly, and if you follow the recommended structures for the preparation of the plan you will naturally have to analyse your market and your competition. Having prepared all of this, you still need to bear in mind that decisions are often made emotionally and justified with logic – so please get external opinions on your business plan to help you ensure that the plan is complete and that you do not have any blind spots in your thinking.

The business plan is also used by external third parties to appraise the business and ensure that you have fully considered all areas. Perhaps the most obvious is your bank manager, who will use the contents of the plan to ensure that the proposition for funding is viable; however, any ethical franchisor will also want to see the plan that you prepare, and more importantly ensure that you have considered everything in both the wording of the plan and the financial projections, as it will give the franchisor a guide as to your commercial acumen.

The plan also provides an excellent accountability tool for you to monitor the progress of the franchise once you start trading. Within a typical business plan, as detailed later in this chapter, there are a number of financial projections that you can then track actual performance against to ensure that you are hitting your budgets. Business plans should also identify and quantify the main non-financial KPIs (key performance indicators) of the franchise, which can also be tracked during this process.

While preparing a plan, it is vital that you are as honest as possible during the process. The typical user of a business plan (investor, bank manager, etc) will be playing devil's advocate, and looking for opportunities to highlight areas where you could have been more prudent, or perhaps have missed a vital risk to your franchise. These weaknesses in a plan might damage the overall perception that they have of you as a business owner, and might cause them to investigate further for other discrepancies. Therefore, I would always suggest that you provide a fair and balanced view of both the opportunities and the risks.

Remember this: Advice from a franchisor

Your business plan is a key part of your overall assessment of the business opportunity. **It's your chance to challenge yourself and be challenged by others.** Be sure to put sufficient time and effort into developing this document and the associated projections as it will be your yardstick for evaluating future performance. **Most franchisors will provide you with a templated profit and loss account and cash flow forecasts that are tailored to their business; but it is for you to test projections yourself.** Benchmark these against information available from your franchisor in terms of what has been previously achieved in a similar franchise. If you're not confident in finance and accounting, preparation of this plan can be outsourced, but make sure you understand it, as you will be questioned on it by the franchisor and by others such as a bank that may be providing finance.

Mike Parker, franchisor Minster Cleaning Services

Who should prepare a business plan?

Many people are daunted by the prospect of preparing a business plan, as it is a document that most people would only ever prepare once or twice in their life, if at all. Although many accountants offer a 'business plan' service, I would strongly recommend against this, and instead simply use them to review a plan prepared by you, and to prepare/review the financial information. It is important that the business plan reflects you and your franchise, and I believe that it can only work as a self-appraisal exercise if the prospective franchisee has a significant involvement in its preparation.

You might also find that your franchisor offers you a 'template business plan'. These templates can range insofar as the level of completion, with perhaps the worst-case scenario being that the franchisor has already completed it for you, depriving you of the opportunity to really grasp the business and appraise whether it is right for you. While template business plans are great as they can guide you in the right direction, a pre-completed plan is really no more than an extension of the sales literature from a franchisor and should raise alarm bells!

The final option, and in my opinion the best option, is to engage the assistance of a specialist business plan preparer, such as Franchise Finance (www.franchisefinance.co.uk/), and be actively involved in the process. Being staffed by former bank managers, they know exactly how to present the business plan to the bank; however, they will also be working in your favour due to the way that they charge (on a small percentage of successful funding achieved). As they are known by all of the franchise banks, they are also unlikely to submit an unrealistic plan as they would not want to jeopardize these relationships, so you will also have a degree of independence in the preparation of the plan.

How long should a business plan be?

A business plan can range from one sheet of A4 through to hundreds of pages; however, for a typical franchise I expect to see plans of between 15 and 25 pages. This is broadly divided equally between the 'words' and the 'numbers' insofar as content is concerned. The key for any business plan is to ensure that you can get your point across fully and clearly, while not overwhelming the reader with superfluous detail.

There is no standard format for a business plan; however, I'd suggest that you choose a common font in a readable size so that it can be viewed on both Macs and PCs. I would also steer clear of using too many different fonts, colours and sizes. They say 'a picture is worth a thousand words', and for a business that is reliant on a visual experience (say retail, or product franchises), a well-placed visual can often communicate your ideas far better than text ever could.

What should a business plan include?

When putting together a business plan you should remember that there is no fixed structure of a plan – these documents vary from business to business; however, there is a level of expectation from the reader of the plan.

Normally, I would expect to see the following areas covered within a business plan:

► Executive summary

► Business briefing

► Market review

► SWOT analysis

► Background of the business owner

► Funding briefing

► Financial information.

As mentioned before, your franchisor may have a template business plan document for you to use. Alternatively, most of the high street banks also have these templates available. Before approaching your bank, it is vital that you read the next chapter on funding to understand how the franchise departments work in each bank, as the process differs slightly from standard business banking.

Executive summary

Cutting through the technical jargon, the executive summary should be a concise summary of who you are, what the business needs in respect of funding, and how you are going to pay it back. This summary prepares the reader for what the plan should include, and provides a 'big picture' reference point for when they have to dive into the detail. It should only be approximately one page long.

An important point to note is that most bank managers and other funders receive several business plans each week. They have an obligation to read through the whole plan before committing to funding, so from their perspective less is often more! Of course you need to ensure that you cover all of the expected points, and raise everything that the manager needs to be aware of; however, by being brief where possible you will make the reader's life a lot easier. As I mentioned earlier, striking the right balance between providing all necessary details and overwhelming the reader is essential.

Business briefing

This is where you should provide details of what the franchise is, how it will operate, which sectors it will operate in, the territory that you are purchasing, and the highlights of the financial projections. I would tend to cap this to one or two pages, and also include comprehensive details about who the franchisor is, and some background on the existing network.

This section isn't the place to go into any detail about your competitive advantage; however, a broad summary of why your business would outperform others is worth including. Also, any relevant experience or knowledge, or indeed transferable skills that you have are worth mentioning here.

Market review

In this section, you should include details of the market research that you have carried out concerning the business. This will include local competition, both from national franchises and smaller independent operators. The reader of the business plan wants to ensure that you have considered all aspects of the marketplace, including competition that isn't as obvious as your direct competitors.

This is the point where you set out full details of the territory that you are purchasing, and confirm whether it is exclusive or non-exclusive. If your franchisor has provided you with any demographic data on your region, this is also valuable information that will help the user of the business plan understand the likely demand for your business.

Other things that you can do to give some clarity on local demand may include desk research, footfall analysis, and general feedback from the local area. I would expect to see both quantitative and qualitative information in this section, and a clear explanation of what sets the business apart from its competitors in the marketplace.

SWOT analysis

A SWOT analysis is very simply an analysis of your business: its

▶ Strengths

▶ Weaknesses

▶ Opportunities

▶ Threats.

These should be honestly appraised and included within the business plan. When preparing this analysis it is important to remember that 'strengths' and 'weaknesses' are internal, but 'opportunities' and 'threats' are external. Certainly, when I advise business owners I tend to review this section to see how honestly and openly they are describing the business and themselves, since it allows me to form an opinion on the validity of the remainder of the plan and their pitch.

Background of the business owner

For me, this is one of the key parts of the plan. Although the franchise is its own entity so far as the business plan is concerned, it will flourish or fail depending on the skills and qualities that the franchisee behind it has.

As mentioned in previous chapters, one of the key things to highlight is any transferable experience that you have. This may be directly related to the business – for example, if you were employed as an estate agent and then decide to purchase an estate agency franchise. However, it may be that you are entering into a new area, in which case you should highlight the skills that you have acquired previously. These may include:

▶ **sales** skills

▶ **team leadership** skills

▶ **financial** skills

▶ **administration** skills.

It is also wise to include a brief CV within the business plan, since many banks request this as part of their process.

Funding briefing

Potential funders want to understand how much they are being asked for, and what the return is for them. This part of the plan should elaborate on the earlier funding narrative by drilling into the detail of what exactly the funds would be used for – whether initial capital costs or for working capital.

A lender also expects to see consideration of the funding mix, to show how the proposed deal should look.

Financial information

This is the part of the plan where you will provide evidence for the claims made within your previous briefings, and is often the section that startups need advice on. There are various components to the financial section, including:

▶ **Projected Profit & Loss Accounts** – typically these projections would be prepared on a monthly basis, for the first three years of the business.

▶ **Projected Balance Sheets** – again, these would typically be prepared for the first three years; however, depending on the type of business, it may be for quarterly or annual periods rather than monthly.

▶ **Cash Flow Projections** – these would be required on a monthly basis, demonstrating the cash flows of the business.

One common mistake that many new business owners make is not understanding the difference between cash flow forecasts and profit & loss forecasts. When trading in business there are a number of 'non-cash' items that need to be included within the financial information of the business, such as depreciation. There are also cash items that might not be reflected within the profit & loss of the company, such as capital investment.

My strong recommendation for all potential franchisees is to take professional advice on the preparation of the financial information, as this is the area that banks and other funding institutions look to investigate thoroughly.

Dos and don'ts of writing a business plan

There are some basic rules when it comes to writing a business plan, which can save you a lot of wasted time and embarrassment:

▶ **DO** write in clear English.

▶ **DO** make sure that your executive summary is clear and covers all necessary areas.

▶ **DO** make sure that your plan is provided in both hard copy and computerized formats.

▶ **DO** make sure that you take professional advice where needed.

▶ **DON'T** use fancy fonts or overwhelming pictures – the user of the plan wants you to get to the point.

▶ **DON'T** over-engineer the plan – most readers want to get the information they need as quickly as possible.

▶ **DON'T** scrimp on the quality of the final document – use decent quality paper, and make sure that the plan is bound in an appropriate fashion.

▶ **DON'T** abdicate responsibility for your plan; it is essential that you have some input into the document so that you can talk about it credibly, and so that you can provide reassurance that the plan is realistic.

Where to get advice on business plans

Preparing a business plan can seem like a solitary job, but there are plenty of resources out there to help you if you need guidance after reading this chapter.

BANK MANAGER

Although you will be approaching a bank manager with your business plan, often the banks have template plans to give you some guidance as to how they should be prepared. Make sure that you speak to your manager during the process of applying for funding. They have a vested interest in providing funding, since it will be likely to make up part of their targets; but they also need to ensure that the bank's money is used responsibly.

We'll discuss more about the process of raising funds in the next chapter.

ACCOUNTANT

A qualified accountant will be able to help you create and validate your financial projections, and can provide input into the best ways to fund your business. You should therefore hire an accountant to at least review the projections that you have made. If an accountant has been used during the preparation of the plan, it would be worth making note of this in the plan so that the banks have the assurance that professional advice has been sought.

There's a benefit to engaging a specialist franchise accountant at this stage since he or she may well look after other franchisees within your network, or at least franchisees of similar networks, and hence will be able to provide you with feedback based on their experiences of dealing with similar franchises.

FINANCE BROKER

If you are using a finance broker to assist you with obtaining finance, he or she will naturally want to help you with the preparation of the plan. A specialist within the franchising industry will also have experience of dealing with other franchisees in a similar or even the same network; and as such will be a valued adviser, much like a franchise accountant.

BUSINESS COLLEAGUES

Any friends or colleagues that you may have who are currently in business can often provide you with a useful sounding board for the ideas in your business plan, and can help you by casting a critical eye over the draft document before you finalize it.

If they are commercially minded, their help would be especially valuable in reviewing the competitor analysis and your unique selling points (USPs). Ideally, ask them to take the role of a bank manager to see if they would lend you money based on the strength of your plan.

ONLINE GUIDES

There is also a plethora of online guides out there to help you build a business plan. A great resource is www.bplans.co.uk, which provides a range of business plan templates to help you get started. You will also find a fantastic resource on http://www.greatbusiness.gov.uk/the-how-to-write-a-business-plan-guide/, which consolidates the various sources of business plan templates, and articles/checklists from the banks and other useful organizations.

What does a franchisor look for?

It's important to always bear in mind that when preparing a business plan for a new franchise, the bank isn't your only recipient. Any decent franchisor will take an active interest in the business plan, much in the same way that it will take an interest in the performance of your business going forwards.

The franchisor will be looking through your plan to ensure that you fully understand the business that you are entering into, and that you are realistic with your expectations from day one. If they sense that you are estimating higher than realistic levels of turnover and profit, most ethical franchisors would look to rein in your expectations at this stage, to avoid disputes down the line. They are also looking to see how you approach competitor research, etc, as this will give them a strong indication of your business acumen.

Remember this: Advice from a franchisor

As a franchisor I am looking for eight key sections, covering everything from their understanding of the concept through to a full financial breakdown. Primarily the business plan has to be theirs and theirs alone; many franchisors will give prospective franchisees help in creating their business plan but at the end of the day it's the franchisee who is borrowing the money, who's taking the risk and ultimately who has to pay the bills.

The main sections I am looking out for are:

Outline – What is the principle of the franchise business. This shows me an understanding of the company and that they have thoroughly researched the market.

Product or service – Precisely what is the business going to offer its customers? What are the main selling points of the business and how do they differ from the competition? What's the point of difference?

People – Who are the principals in the business, who is going to be driving the business forward and what is his or her background and relevant experience? CVs of individuals help me a great deal here.

Market – This is the most important section of the whole plan. Without a clear understanding of the market the business will not succeed. If franchisees can show me that they have done their homework and researched every possible avenue, then that is a big tick for me against their suitability. In this section I would expect to see facts and figures, current market conditions, who will their main targets be and who are the competitors? And, ultimately, why would customers choose your product or service over that of your competitors?

Marketing plan – If you don't know where you are going then any road will take you there! This is so true. Without a credible marketing plan then how are you going to win those new customers? Within this segment I am looking for indicators of their planned market share and number of sales. Also what marketing collateral are they going to use – is it mailshots, media advertising or social media. Have they spoken to any potential customers already and tested the market? Prove to me there is a need for the product or service in the location.

Premises – Where will the business operate from and what are the costs involved? Clearly the franchisor will have a steer on this but it's good to see that the prospect has researched what is available and the suitability. Points to consider are location, footfall (if it's a retail business), running costs, any planning restrictions and, of course, whether the premises allow your business to grow and develop without short-term relocation.

Financial information – Start with a summary of key facts, i.e. the financial forecast. Will you make a profit or loss in the first 12 months? Does this business require startup funding? If so, how much and where from? What is the breakeven point of the business – what value of sales do you have to make each week/month to cover the running costs of your business? Equally, I am keen to see the prospects' expectations in terms of running their home, how much do they need to take out each month to live?

I'm also keenly interested in the cash flow forecast. How much cash does this business require to cover the delay between purchasing materials and receiving payments from its customers? I have seen this cause so many issues in businesses that on the surface seem profitable – yet fail due to insufficient cash flow.

Dave Galvin, franchisor Dwyer Group (UK)

Focus points

✳ A business plan is not just for the bank manager! It is a useful self-appraisal process, helping you determine whether the business is right for you.

✳ You should take professional advice; however, you must 'own the plan' and understand its contents.

✳ Make sure that the plan is easily understood by its readership.

✳ A good plan is honest and explains both the strengths and weaknesses of the business.

✳ A good plan also includes both details on the business and detailed financial projections to substantiate any claims.

Next step

In this chapter we've looked at what the business plan is, and broadly what it should contain. One of the main users of a business plan is a potential funder, and in the next chapter we will explore how you can obtain funding.

13

Arranging funding and bank facilities

In this chapter you will learn:

▶ *The types of funding available*
▶ *How to get a lender to say yes*
▶ *What a bank looks for when you approach it.*

Once you have a business plan organized, you need to work out how you are going to fund the franchise. This area can be relatively simple, for example, if you are investing in a franchise after receiving redundancy pay or an inheritance. However, for many it involves some level of external funding.

Fortunately, as we are now out of the last recession, we have a great position in that banks are willing to lend money, and there are alternative lending sources available if required.

Personal investment

Given that there is no external lender to satisfy, this route is certainly the 'easiest' insofar as administration and minimum application requirements; however, you need to consider whether you have sufficient finances to run the business and maintain a contingency fund should it be required (let's say if the franchise isn't as successful as projected, or your partner is made redundant, etc).

Even though there is no application process, or any difficult questions to be answered, I would urge you to ensure that you still go through the process of preparing a comprehensive business plan to make sure that the business is right for you.

It is always important to make sure that your spouse or partner (if you have one) is as committed to the business as you, and that he or she is happy to use personal funds if this is the route that you choose. There are very few things that are more frustrating than hearing 'I told you so' after a failed business investment!

Family loans

Family loans are often a popular choice with many potential franchisees when available as there are (usually!) no formal application procedures or credit checks. I would strongly recommend that anyone choosing this route prepares a properly drafted agreement, so that the terms of the loan are clear from the outset. I would also suggest that both sides consider how they will deal with the worst-case scenario of the business failing, both financially and personally.

Family loans rarely have a typical structure, and I've seen cases of both interest and non-interest bearing loans, with a range of repayment deals. Regardless of how the loan looks, and regardless of how well you get along with each other at the moment, it is vital that the loan is documented to protect both sides.

Bank loans

Despite the generally gloomy news that circulates in the media, most high street banks are willing to lend money to franchisees on enhanced terms compared to independent startups. In fact, it's easy to forget that lending money is one of the reasons why they are in business!

Even though there is money to lend, and a variety of government- and bank-led initiatives (such as Funding for Lending, Enterprise Finance Guarantee scheme, and various industry funds), it's important to approach the bank in a professional and knowledgeable fashion. Make sure that you fully understand the detail of your business plan, and can answer any questions confidently and consistently.

As a rule of thumb at the time of publishing, banks will typically meet 50 per cent of the funding requirement for a general startup, and as mentioned earlier some banks in the franchising sector will extend to 70 per cent for a recognized, established franchise. There are usually arrangement fees in addition to interest, and you must also consider any covenants (restrictions and/or requirements) that might be placed on you while the lending facility is in place.

Personal loans/remortgaging

When investigating financing for a business, particularly if it is a smaller franchise, always consider the option of raising funds personally. Often, the interest rates for an unsecured personal loan are lower than those for a business loan. There are also no arrangement fees, and potentially other perks such as gift vouchers/reward points offered as new customer incentives.

Remortgaging a property is another option for raising funds. The interest is usually lower than that charged on a personal or business loan, and the repayment terms can be far longer. It is vital, however, to ensure that both you (and your life partner) are happy to put your property up as security for the bank.

Overdrafts

Overdrafts are often used to fund working capital, where a 'floating' facility is needed. There is no formal capital repayment schedule as with structured finance such as a loan; however, remember that an overdraft is technically repayable on demand.

Again, as with bank loans there is typically an arrangement fee, calculated as a percentage of the facility, together with an interest charge for the amount of overdraft used within the period. The facility may also be subject to covenants, which are terms that the business must adhere to in order to continue to qualify for the overdraft.

Leasing/hire purchase arrangements

For asset purchases, it is often prudent to consider whether the item can be purchased using a lease or a hire purchase agreement, which is itself secured against the asset.

There are two types of leases – **operating leases** and **finance leases**. They have different accounting treatments, and fundamentally with an operating lease you are merely 'renting' the item, whereas with a finance lease you are 'purchasing' the item. Make sure that you get clarity on the type of lease before entering into any commitment.

Banks will look for you to consider these arrangements when you are looking to fund a franchise with capital assets, since it spreads the funding risk for them.

Peer-to-peer lending/crowdfunding

Peer-to-peer lending is a relatively new way to access finance, facilitated by websites such as Zopa (http://www.zopa.com/).

It allows members of the general public to invest their money into these loans, acting as a brokerage (much in the same way that Betfair adapted the traditional bookmakers model by allowing customers to bet for and lay against each side). The broker will typically take a lending fee, which is deducted from the interest rate charged by the lender to the business.

This is a funding avenue that is open to most individuals with a good credit history, and this market is developing at a rapid rate. As it is a new approach, there haven't been too many horror stories in the press about peer-to-peer lending; however, this might change as the market develops.

Crowdfunding is also another new way to access finance, and as with peer-to-peer lending it is relatively untested in the franchise market. One consideration to bear in mind is that your franchisor will want a contractual arrangement with just one person, not a collection of investors, and it is important that you ensure your franchisor is satisfied with the funding model that you choose to use.

Key idea: Advice from an expert

In simple terms, there are two important factors about funding a franchise business. The first is calculating the right amount of money that you will need and the second is being able to persuade a lender (or lenders) to lend it to you.

So firstly, '**businesses go bust when they run out of money**' and while estimating the level of year-end projected profit is important, estimating the amount of actual cash that you will need on top of your startup costs i.e. the additional working capital to cover overheads, etc. in order to actually get to the end of the year, is even more important. A correctly produced set of financial projections, based on average historic performance levels within the network, will enable the total financial requirement to be calculated.

The next step is to find a willing lender. The following banks all have a franchise department and are keen to lend where the network has a proven track record of profitable franchisees in the UK: Allied Irish Bank, HSBC, Lloyds, Metro Bank, NatWest and RBS.

These banks have varying appetites for different sectors but are generally willing to lend between 50 per cent and 70 per cent of the total amount required (startup costs, working capital and VAT). They normally want some sort of security, e.g. a 1st or 2nd charge over property if the borrowing is more than £25,000/£30,000. If this is not available then the Government's Enterprise Finance Guarantee Scheme can, in certain circumstances, provide the necessary collateral.

Where a proportion of the funding requirement relates to things like vans, equipment and machinery, it is often better to take this on what is known as 'asset finance' from a leasing company. While probably more expensive it means that the franchisee will have the 'bandwidth' to borrow more overall, thus maximizing the amount of available crucial working capital from the bank in the first few years of trading.

The way to get lenders to say 'yes' is to provide them with a professional business plan that clearly shows what the franchisee is going to do, how they are going to do it, how much money they are going to need and make, and how and when the lender/s are going to be repaid. In addition to this they need to demonstrate that they have a good credit history and that the business will be able to provide sufficient drawings to cover their personal/family monthly living expenses.

The further removed from the ideal scenario painted above any particular franchisee's individual case is, the harder it will be to borrow money. Having said that, there is a second tier of lenders in the UK who are becoming increasingly interested in franchising but will probably charge higher rates, e.g. in excess of 10 per cent, and it will therefore be necessary to ensure that the business model can sustain this type of funding.

Chris Roberts, director Franchise Finance

Key idea: Advice from a bank

So you have completed your business plan and you have an appointment with the bank to discuss the support you need. What do you need to consider?

✵ **Be prepared**; perhaps even practise with your wife/husband/friends what you are going to say.

* **Arrive on time and be appropriately dressed.** Being on time creates a good first impression and dress according to the business. So if you are going to be a consultant, dress in a suit, though a tie is no longer necessary. If the business is more manual, a suit is not necessary but be smart/presentable nonetheless.
* **Be passionate, positive and personable** and try not to be nervous.
* **Can you summarize your business plan**, perhaps with a mission statement that you can expand on to include a brief assessment of your strengths, weaknesses, etc. Understanding your weaknesses and business threats are a positive for the manager. You need to know your business plan, especially the key numbers such as sales, profit and break-even, and be able to explain how they have been arrived at e.g. 'X number of sales at £Y = turnover'.
* **Ensure you have considered the personal drawings you need**, if you have no other personal income, and does the profit in the business allow for this amount to be taken out?
* **Make sure there are no spelling mistakes in the plan** or in any spreadsheet formulas that do not add up – **give the numbers a sense check**.
* **Expect the bank manager to challenge your assumptions** and consider what they might be. For example, they may ask 'what if' type questions around sales, and what the family feels about the venture.
* **Think about the competition in your market** and be able to explain in detail your own USPs. Take care, though, not to criticize the competition, since they may be respected customers of the bank.
* **Try to avoid industry jargon** in the plan or in your conversation. You may know the acronyms but will the bank manager know these?
* **Comment about any research you have done** to establish the franchisor's brand.
* **Have you had any other third-party involvement**, such as an accountant?
* **How can the bank manager help you?** – Is there more they can do to help your business other than provide the finance? Could they become a customer and can you incentivize them to do so? They can then recommend your service to other customers, friends and family.

Mark Scott, director (franchising) NatWest

Focus points

* ✶ Don't just think about bank loans – think about all the possible options for funding your franchise.
* ✶ If you have personal funds available, an external funder would be expecting you to have 'skin in the game'.
* ✶ If you are not an ideal candidate for lending, there are still options available; however, these may be more expensive.
* ✶ Approach the meeting with your bank manager in a professional manner.
* ✶ Remember, you should be speaking to your bank's franchise team, not just a local small business manager, since they will know your network and may be able to offer 70 per cent funding rather than standard ratios.

Next step

In this chapter we've explored how you can take your business plan and use it to successfully obtain funding. The next chapter will cover the minefield that is property selection.

14

Finding business premises

In this chapter you will learn:

▶ *What support the franchisor should give you*
▶ *How to work effectively from home if needed*
▶ *From a real-life example of business property support requirements.*

One of the major stumbling blocks in starting a franchise is finding suitable premises. It may be that the franchise that you are buying is a 'home-based' franchise, in which case other than making sure that you are set up appropriately (see below), you are fairly free of problems in this area. If, however, you are looking to find retail premises, there is a whole world of challenges ahead!

Key idea: Advice from an expert

Are you left alone in this? Ideally you shouldn't be, especially if this is your first experience of negotiating leases, obtaining planning permission and project managing building works.

Most premises-based franchisors will have a team with experience in all of these aspects ready to guide you, and (unless you are very experienced in such matters) you would be well advised to let them handle this on your behalf, as they will doubtless have been through this dozens of times and recognize the pitfalls.

The process can usually be broken down into five separate stages:

* Locating the premises
* Investigating the suitability of the site
* Negotiating the terms of the lease
* Obtaining planning permission for your proposed usage
* Project managing the building works or fit-out.

Location, Location, Location...

Dealing with the first point on the list, the difficulty of finding suitable premises depends very much upon what sort of business you are looking to open. You may just require a 'high street presence', but again you need to know that you're at the right end of the right high street before signing any leases. This comes back to the market research that you will have performed as part of your business plan. So, first of all, you need to know you're in the right place.

What the site offers

You may have other requirements to do with parking, access, licensing hours, fume extraction or a multitude of other factors, all of which can conspire to make the search for the 'right' premises frustratingly difficult. Many franchisors retain search agents who know exactly what size, style and type of premises are needed, and will run national marketing campaigns to find them. You are of course welcome to help with the search since local knowledge can be a huge help, but make sure that you have discussed this with the franchisor in detail so that you know exactly what you are looking for and don't duplicate the agents' efforts.

Negotiating the lease

You may also be surprised to find that (assuming you are operating as a new-start business) many landlords will be reluctant to take you on as their tenant because, in their eyes, you represent a very high risk. This is usually because the landlord worries that you have no previous experience in the sector and assumes that you will not therefore have much chance of success. This is usually the sign of a landlord who doesn't understand franchising!

A helpful franchisor, with a track record of success, will often get involved in the discussions with the landlord, pointing out that franchised businesses historically have a much greater success rate and also explaining how the franchisor will be as committed to the success of the project as the franchisee.

Very often, the franchisor will enter into a Deed of Option with the landlord, which gives them the rights (although not usually the obligation) to take over the premises if the tenant were to leave for any reason. This can offer reassurances to the landlord. In other cases, the franchisor may take on the lease, and then sub-let the premises to you. In certain instances this may be the only way to get a landlord to let high-value premises to new franchisees, and while it is generally a good thing, you must remember that even though your franchisor will be your landlord, the terms of the lease will remain the same and they will not tolerate any missed or late rent payments just because they know you!

Planning permission

Different businesses require different categories of planning permission, defined using a somewhat-random alphanumeric scale (category A1 is Retail, A3 is Food & drink, D2 is Leisure usage, and so on). You need to be sure that your chosen premises either have, or have the potential to obtain, the correct category of planning permission for their proposed usage. It is crucial that qualified (and insured) advice is taken before planning applications are submitted, and your franchisor should either have its own advisers or be able to direct you towards suitably qualified professionals to handle this work for you. Very often it's not about what you say in a planning application, but more about the way in which you say it!

Premises fit-out

The franchisor will usually have very specific rules regarding the fit-out, which often requires some modifications to the layout of the premises. Franchisors will typically specify the equipment that should be installed, the colours of walls, the materials used for floorcoverings and furniture, and so on. Don't be surprised if you are not allowed any input into this – franchising is all about making sure the customers' expectations of the brand are consistently met, so just because you don't like the colour of the carpet they have specified, doesn't mean you can change it!

There are many pitfalls for the unwary in handling even seemingly modest fit-out projects. If you try to fit some toilets against a wall that has no plumbing services connected, then you could incur significant extra costs which a little more planning could have avoided. Unless you are experienced in identifying the run of pipeworks and drainage hidden underfloor this would be an easy mistake to make. Again, your franchisor will almost certainly have preferred contractors who have done its sites before, or will provide a specification document with which you can brief your own contractors, but if you are not sure about any aspect of this it is far safer to leave it to the franchisor. There is a temptation to assume that the franchisor will be 'marking up' the building works (although in practice this is rare – they usually seek to make their money much further down the line, and don't want to burden their franchisees with inflated startup costs) and so it is a natural instinct to want to handle this yourself to save money, but you will often find that as you won't have the buying power or experience of the franchisor this turns into a false economy.

Steve Felmingham, former franchise consultant and franchisor, Banana Moon Day Nurseries

Home-based franchises

It may be that you are able to run your franchise from home to begin with, and if so you are probably breathing a sigh of relief having read the above issues that property-based franchisees have to overcome!

While operating from home is a simpler way of starting, and certainly incurs lower costs in the early days, there are some factors that you do need to consider to ensure that the working arrangements are appropriate for both you and your family:

▶ Is your franchisor happy that the business can be presented adequately from your own premises?

▶ Do you have a work space free from distractions?

▶ In truth, will you be able to be committed to working from home if there are household chores that need doing?

▶ Will you be able to work effectively on your own, or do you prefer to have others around you (in which case, a shared office space might be more suitable)?

▶ Are you allowed to operate from home under your insurance policy?

▶ Do you need to advise the local authority about your use of home as a business premises?

▶ Are you sure that you will be able to create sufficient separation between your home life and your business life?

▶ If you will have business visitors, do you have sufficient parking and will your home present the right image to them?

▶ Will your neighbours be happy with the arrangements, and can you be sure that there will be no noisy disturbances while you are trying to work and/or conduct meetings?

Some of these questions might seem obvious, but it is most definitely worth considering them all before deciding to work from home.

Case study: Banana Moon Day Nurseries

Even franchisees who have signed leases or managed projects before have usually not handled every element of this sort of project in the past, and sometimes a little knowledge can be dangerous! For example, when renting basic office space, leases of three or five years are very common. However, our franchisees (in common with many premises-based new franchisees) make a loss in the first year, break-even in the second and only reach a true profit in the third, so even a five-year lease doesn't give them much time to get a return on their investment. Of course, this is very dependent on the type of business. Some businesses can be relocated relatively easily, but in the nursery business suitable premises are extremely hard to find, so it is crucial that the leases are at least ten years (and often much longer). Similarly, we always try to negotiate tenant-only break clauses (which allow the franchisees, but not the landlord, to get out of the lease early). This maximizes flexibility but minimizes risk. We also negotiate caps on rent reviews, again to make sure that the long-term profitability of the business is not eroded by an over-ambitious landlord.

The key thing is that so many aspects are interdependent. The terms of the lease need to reflect the local market conditions, and this can only be established by doing detailed market research and then drawing up a full business plan. Again, we help with this because it is such a crucial aspect. Only then can the viability of a particular building be assessed. The business plan can also be used as a tool in the landlord negotiations, where we can point out that a certain level of rent is simply not viable, but evidence this with an accurately modelled plan.

We wouldn't expect to leave a franchisee to handle these delicate negotiations since the landlord or agent may not take them seriously and they could easily lose the property or end up agreeing uncompetitive or unsustainable terms.

Then, going on from that, finding buildings with the correct category of planning permission for a nursery (Category D1) is notoriously difficult, so it invariably involves taking on a building in a different category and applying for 'Change of Use'. This means that we need to assess the building initially for the likelihood of obtaining the requisite 'Change of Use' and, assuming this looks reasonably certain of success, then preparing a detailed and well-reasoned planning application. Again, a poorly drafted application is unlikely to be successful, so we handle all of that for our franchisees as part of the franchise package.

We then face the challenge of keeping the landlord 'onside' while the planning application goes through. This takes a minimum of eight weeks during which time the landlord is just waiting to hear if you will actually be taking the building, and many get disheartened and start looking for another tenant unless you are in regular contact, keeping the tenant updated. So, again, we keep a dialogue going.

Even with a successful 'Change of Use' the permission may have conditions applied, such as the amount of space given over to car parking, or the extent of structural change that will be permitted and in some cases this may mean re-visiting the business plan to make sure the business model is still viable.

Sometimes we will be going back to the landlord for a contribution towards any additional costs arising as a result of these conditions.

Then we get to the building works; these will vary dramatically depending upon the size and style of the building and its previous use (our nurseries have been housed in everything from former offices, restaurants, libraries and doctors' surgeries to pubs and churches in the past). We usually have to re-position some walls as we are bound by complex legislation regarding floorspace per child, and the movement of a wall just one metre in one direction can sometimes make a huge difference to the potential profitability of the setting.

We also have to install infant toilets, fit a kitchen, install air conditioning, create disabled access, install CCTV, build a playground and comply with myriad Health & Safety and OFSTED requirements. We need the final result to be safe, bright and fun, but also to have the elements that make it recognizably a Banana Moon nursery. This sometime means difficult conversations with franchisees who would love to put their own touches to it, but we have to respect the customers of the brand who have certain expectations and, perhaps more importantly, we just want to protect franchisees from getting it wrong! We have seen too many cases in the past where a franchisee has asked a builder to position something in a particular place during the build, and we have to come back and re-position it for reasons that the franchisee wouldn't have the experience to anticipate!

In the midst of all of this it is easy for a franchisee to forget why he or she bought a franchise: to benefit from the franchisor's well-known and recognizable brand, and to avoid going through a learning curve whilst finding out the hard way what works and what doesn't. If we have one piece of advice for any potential franchisee it would always be this: listen to your franchisor, who is as committed as you to making a success of the project, and will have made all of the mistakes over the years so that you don't have to!

Steve Felmingham, franchisor Banana Moon Day Nurseries

In summary, all I can say about property selection and negotiation is that it could form the basis of a book in itself! Your franchisor should be able to help you through this minefield, such as in the case study above, and as such it's vital that you call on support and – more to the point – make sure that the franchisor you choose is willing to offer such support.

Focus points

* Your franchisor should have done this several times before, and can provide you with a wealth of experience.
* In particular, you can expect a franchisor to support you in the negotiations with your landlord, and the planning process.
* Your franchisor will also know what to look for in premises.
* If you are working from home, you need to make sure that the workspace will be suitable for both your home and business life.

Next step

In this chapter we have covered many areas on premises selection, with the help of some expert guidance from Steve Felmingham. Next, we will look at how franchising is different from running an independent business (and from employment).

Part Five

Starting the franchise

How is franchising different?

In this chapter you will learn:

► *How franchising is different to employment*
► *How franchising is different to running an independent business*
► *Some pros and cons of running a franchise.*

A question that I'm often asked when speaking to people who don't understand franchising is 'how is franchising different'. As you can imagine, this question in itself is very open, and I believe better summarized by two different questions:

▶ How is franchising different to employment?

▶ How is franchising different to running your own independent business?

Now, the first question might seem to be far easier to answer than the second; however, the reality is that some franchises lend themselves more to a controlled operational role, and others lend themselves more towards a hands-off approach by the franchisor. In reality, the best option is the one that is best for you as a franchisee, having weighed up your own skills set and the support infrastructure provided by the franchisor.

You might remember that in Chapter 3 (Who makes a good franchisee?), I touched upon the differences between networks in relation to how they deal with their franchisees and the level of control exerted over the individuals working in their networks. The fact that we have these differences between franchisors means that the question of how franchising is different from either employment or running your own independent business is fairly difficult to answer.

By way of example, there is a home services franchise that I know of that charges its self-employed cleaners a very low fixed management service fee of a couple of hundred pounds per month. In return, the franchisee receives a listing on its (well-marketed) website, a manual and an agreement – there is relatively little by way of support. On the other hand, there is a business-to-business franchise that I know of that provides all of the marketing collateral, actually does the work for the franchisee, and manages the administration of the business – the franchisee is almost a distributor, and in turn pays a significant amount to the franchisor in total. Because we have no legal definition of what constitutes a franchise agreement versus what constitutes a distribution or licensing agreement, both businesses are valid business format franchise models, yet are suitable for different people due to the differing level of support from the head office insofar as running the business and actually fulfilling the customer need.

I would place the two examples above at the opposite ends of the spectrum, with one being more akin to non-franchised self-employment (albeit with a brand and a manual), and the other being controlled, monitored and supported more like an employed role. Having said that, most franchises tend to lie somewhere in between these two extremes.

So, even in the most supported 'employment'-style franchise, how does it differ from true employment?

1 As a franchisee you have ultimate control over your working life, subject to the obligations within the franchise agreement and operations manual.

2 As a franchisee you are generally in control of your own income levels.

3 As a franchisee you can choose the customers that you deal with.

4 As a franchisee you are *not* entitled to employment benefits such as paid holiday pay or sick pay.

5 As a franchisee you are not entitled to the protection afforded to employees under employment legislation.

6 As a franchisee you are not responsible for your own tax liabilities.

7 As a franchisee there is no guarantee of a fixed income (apart from the very few franchise models that guarantee a level of turnover – not profit – for the franchisee, derived from head office contracts).

While the above is a snapshot of the main differences, the underlying theme is responsibility. As a franchisee, you are responsible for yourself, your business, your staff (if you have any) and indeed your customers' experiences.

Now we come to the difference between franchising and running your own business. I've very deliberately steered away from using the term 'self-employment' since it gives the impression of a solitary self-employed role, whereas many franchises offer a great opportunity for building a larger business with staff.

The biggest difference between franchising and running your own business is that, in an ideal world, a franchise is a 'business in a box'. As part of your initial investment, you receive a blueprint that sets out exactly how you can build and run the business; a brand that has some protection and traction; and a head office team that can support you in your new business.

Remember this: Advice from a franchisor

One of the hardest things about being self-employed and getting a business off the ground is getting your name out there in the market – be it a product, service or both, getting people to know about your existence comes at a high cost.

A massive benefit of franchising is that in many cases the brand is already recognized, and even if it isn't a household name, or it's a new franchise, the route to market, the sales system and the potential success achievable by following the system is already known. New startups and self-employment doesn't give you this luxury. For example, you try a magazine advert, it doesn't work and it costs you money. A franchisor will already know this; they've tried it!

Phil Harrison, franchisor EnviroVent

Another advantage that cannot be understated is the support from your fellow franchisees. When you enter into a franchise network, you are joining a group of business owners who are very similar to you in that they have made the same decision based on their own personal circumstances, their own interests and their own ambitions. These franchisees have also been there, seen it and done it, so can provide you with useful tips about what works for them, and the practical realities of running a business. They are a great source of information about what is happening around the country, and because of this franchisors tend to run conferences, both annually and regionally during the year, to help facilitate franchisee networking and learning.

You will also find that there is informal networking between franchisees, regardless of whether a franchisor endorses it. I'm aware of many franchisee 'closed groups' on social media sites like Facebook where franchisees can share and air their views. These are not always productive, but it is a fact of life that these sites exist. Usually, the networks with a proactive view towards franchisee networking and input, through a combination of conferences and franchise councils (explained later in this book), tend to find that these closed groups and forums are not so much of an issue for their business.

On the flip side, there are downsides in comparison to running an independent business. Perhaps the most obvious downside at first glance is the initial investment and the ongoing management service fee. According to Code of Ethics of the bfa, the initial investment should not be profit making, and instead cover the costs of recruiting and setting up a franchisee in business. The reality is that these costs place an additional burden on the funding requirements of a business, when there are already working capital and potentially asset purchase requirements. Secondly, there is the management service fee, together with any marketing levies, which are required to be paid on a periodic basis. In a well set up franchise, these fees would have been calculated in line with the value provided to you by the franchisor, and will truly be a 'win-win' partnership; however, you do need to be aware that not all franchisors consider this to be a priority! Therefore, it's essential that you do your due diligence on their charging structure to make sure that it is competitive, based on the services provided.

Another downside that might be perceived is the lack of flexibility in how you present yourself and how you do business. As highlighted in the contribution above from Phil Harrison, this is actually a benefit of franchising. A well-established brand should have tried-and-tested processes and systems for you to follow, and any deviation from the process is almost certainly going to be detrimental to you, and possibly the reputation of the network as a whole (with the customers expecting a consistent brand experience). If this does seem like it could be an issue for you, it would be worth reconsidering whether franchising is right for you, since there are certain things that you simply have to adhere to as a franchisee.

Remember this: Advice from a franchisor

You bought a franchise for the proven system so use it. Don't try to reinvent the wheel. The security of a franchise is that the entire network is on the same page, all working towards the same goal, brand message and ethos. Going against the grain to do your own thing can affect brand reputation hugely, especially in this day of social media. You not only affect your own business, you affect others in the network. Stick to the plan.

Anne-Marie Martin, franchisor Diddi Dance

Focus points

✳ Each and every franchise offers a different level of support and obligation, so there is no fixed answer to the question about how a franchise is different.

✳ You need to gauge what support and assistance you need in the business and find a franchise that fits with your requirements.

✳ Even if a network appears to offer a lot of control and support, there will still be substantial differences between running a franchise and being employed.

✳ Generally, running a franchise provides you with a proven system and an established brand, both of which are benefits when compared to running an independent business.

✳ There is also a huge benefit in the support that you can get from fellow franchisees in the network.

Next step

In this chapter we have clarified the difference between a franchise and a non-franchised business. In the next chapter, we will look at how you should set up your business.

16

How to set up your business

In this chapter you will learn:

- ▶ *What the different types of businesses are*
- ▶ *Why a franchisor might dictate certain ways of running your business*
- ▶ *What advice you should take.*

Now that you have an understanding of how franchising is different from setting up an independent business, it's time to consider how to set your business up, and in particular what differences you might encounter in a franchise.

There are various different types of business structure, detailed below. You might find that your franchisor dictates a certain type of structure; which might either be due to its preferred method of doing business (many franchisors insist on their franchisees being limited companies), or due to taxation benefits (many tuition franchisors insist on their franchisees being limited liability partnerships). Other franchisors are happy for you to take external professional advice and decide for yourself!

Sole traders

Possibly the simplest kind of business to run, a sole trade (otherwise known as a sole proprietorship) is a business that is owned by one individual, and from a legal perspective there is no difference between the business and the individual – this is explained in greater depth in the limited company section.

A sole trade can be set up very easily, and only requires minimal form filling to be registered with HM Revenue & Customs. There is no other form filling required, and no requirement to file accounts publicly, so discretion about the business finances is achieved.

Sole trades are referred to by their proprietor's name, and will usually adopt a trading name, such as the following:

Mrs Smith trading as (*or t/a*) ABC Franchise (*location*)

Financially, sole traders have some disadvantages when compared to limited companies (at the time of writing). Firstly, as they are legally considered to have no difference from their owner, the individual would be deemed liable for any business debts, and indeed a business failure could well result in personal bankruptcy.

They also have a different tax treatment to limited companies, in that the entirety of the profit of the business is deemed to be the income of the proprietor for income tax purposes. In brief, the National Insurance that is charged on sole trade profits makes the overall tax burden larger than that of a limited company.

It is important to bear in mind that this difference is proposed to be reduced in 2016 once the 'Dividend Tax' is implemented (at the time of writing, announced in the Chancellor's Autumn Statement).

Partnerships

Partnerships are a combination of more than one trader, and are similar to sole traders except they are owned and operated by more than one person. The partnership would normally have a partnership agreement, which is a legal contract between the business partners about how the business will conduct its day-to-day activities, and also how the partners will deal with any disputes should they arise in the future. If a partnership agreement is not prepared, and no agreement is implied, it is presumed that the terms within the Partnership Act 1890 apply.

Like a sole trade, a partnership is not required to register anywhere except with HM Revenue & Customs, so the startup costs are minimal. They have the same naming situation as sole traders as well, so a typical partnership name may be:

Mrs Smith & Mr Jones trading as ABC Franchise (*location*)

Partnerships have the notion of joint and several liability, as the partnership is deemed to simply be an extension of the individual partners from a legal perspective. As such, there is a risk to all partners in the partnership should the business incur debt. Partnerships are often used for larger businesses than sole trades, and traditionally were used for professional businesses such as architects, doctors' surgeries, accountants and solicitors.

Practically, a franchisor will want to know who is accountable in a franchise agreement, and given the issues when partnerships go wrong, in my experience it will take some persuasion to get the average franchisor to agree to a franchise agreement with a (non-married) partnership!

Limited companies

Although a limited company sounds daunting to those with no experience of running one, they are the most common choice of business vehicle for franchises. From a legal perspective they are seen as being a separate legal entity from the owner(s), and as such can incur debt and own assets in their own right. They also can enter into contracts in their own right, as if they were a 'person'.

A limited company is formed at Companies House, and has its own unique company number and name. No other companies are allowed to use the name of an existing company, and there are also sensitive words that are protected from use. So, for example, the ABC franchise as mentioned above would typically become:

Random Name Limited (*or Ltd*) trading as ABC Franchise (*location*)

A private limited company is run by its directors, who may or may not be the same people as the shareholders (owners). Some companies are set up with the intention of being not-for-profit, and are known as companies limited by guarantee. More commonly for franchises, the company is set up as a company limited by share capital. These companies are often formed for the tax advantages that arise from effective remuneration strategies, and also the commercial advantages of being seen to be a registered limited company.

Limited companies do, however, have two main disadvantages, in that, firstly, they are required to file details of their financial performance and their governance publicly and, secondly, that there is a large administrative burden in the additional requirements of Companies House and the Companies Act.

Limited liability partnership

Limited liability partnerships are a relatively new business structure, introduced in the Limited Liability Partnerships Act 2000. The best way to describe a limited liability partnership (LLP) is as a hybrid between a limited company and a traditional partnership.

Just as with a limited company, a limited liability partnership is formed at Companies House, with its own registration number and unique name. Again, using the ABC Franchise example, a limited liability partnership would be known as:

Random Name LLP trading as ABC Franchise (*location*)

The limited liability partnership would be under the same naming restrictions as a limited company. Again, as with a limited company, it is a separate legal entity in its own right, and can enter into contracts as a legal 'person'. The difference is that a limited liability partnership is made up of members who are much like partners in a partnership. Each limited liability partnership has two designated members who are required to file the accounts for the partnership and to sign the accounts.

Each partner is taxed in the same way as a partner in a partnership, and for VAT purposes the limited liability partnership is deemed to be a partnership, despite being a separate legal entity. There has recently been some legislation passed that puts an additional taxation burden on members who are deemed by HM Revenue & Customs to actually be 'employees'.

Is limited liability really limited?

In short, no!

Your franchisor will look to have a tri-party agreement between itself, you personally, and your business in which you will run the business. This will tie you personally to the obligations and covenants in the agreement. It's likely that banks and other lenders will also look for personal guarantees, effectively removing the limited liability for most significant debts that you could incur.

Deciding which type of business to set up

As you are looking at franchising, I have to admit that this decision is sometimes made for you! Your franchisor might insist on a certain business structure across the network.

If you are left to your own devices, it's best to take advice based on your own personal situation. This advice should cover tax (from an accountant), legal requirements, and also consider the commercial issues that you might encounter.

Focus points

✳ Your franchisor may have a preferred way, or a compulsory way, that you should set your business up.

✳ Even if your franchisor does not enforce a structure, it might be able to point you in the right direction for the structure of your business.

✳ You should take professional advice from an accountant about the best structure from a tax perspective.

✳ If you set up a limited company or a limited liability partnership, you would usually still be expected to sign the franchise agreement personally in addition to on behalf of the company.

Next step

Having looked at the types of business structure available to you, we've completed the theoretical side of running a business. In the next chapter we will look at some case studies from franchisees who have been down the same journey that you are about to embark on...

17

The first day – Case studies

In this chapter you will learn:

▶ *How franchising has been for two different franchisees*
▶ *What the franchisees would do differently*
▶ *The advice that they would give you.*

Below are a couple of case studies from franchisees, highlighting their experiences during the first day and beyond! While I can provide you with anecdotal evidence, these guys have been there, seen it, and lived to tell the tale.

Case study: Betterclean Services

Don't do what I did! Within two months of launch we had landed one of the biggest contracts the franchise network, even the core business, had seen in 18 years of trading! Not only that, what I had landed was not just a significant contract in terms of sales, the margins were VERY healthy too, which is the opposite of what normally happens – bigger contracts = tighter margins! So why was this a bad start...? We were running before we had learned to walk!

Some theory: I believe marketing is about attracting and communicating with defined groups of prospective buyers, understanding their needs and triggers, attracting their interest and guiding them to a transaction. Depending on the objectives of the organization, this will most likely lead to the business making a profit at a defined margin.

The best marketing attracts, educates and engages with your audience, so they enquire ready to buy. They should already understand the value of your offering from the brand and the promotional messaging and may just have a few questions to answer before converting to customers! However others are competing for their attention, so once they become an enquiry they will need nurturing and supporting through the sales process, to hold their interest and build their desire.

Post-purchase, both parties should feel they have a fair deal. The next stage is to continue communicating with your customers, nurturing them to create long, mutually beneficial relationships and encourage them to become recommenders and refers – advocates of your brand!

Marketing covers all communications between all stakeholders... simple!

As a franchisee starting a new business, you want to hit the ground running, as I did back in 2013! Your franchisor should provide you with a proven launch marketing strategy, which will most likely commence way before your actual 'launch'! Of course the marketing activities within the plan/schedule will take many forms, totally depending on the target audiences. Often there is a focus on building awareness of the new business in the local area, as well as attracting prospective customers! The flyers, adverts, editorials, PPC campaigns, even the marketing plan, should have all been refined over many launches before, assuming you are not a pilot franchisee! Therefore starting a business with a franchise should mean that you receive a proven template launch marketing strategy, a marketing plan, supporting collateral and of course some physical guidance and support!

So, if you follow the model, how can you fail?

The key areas that you need to be aware of:

* Understand the strategy and plan
* Embrace the activities in the schedule
* Implement the plan and check you are doing so as intended!

The key to these points is following the model. And to repeat this again, it is your responsibility as franchisee to ensure you understand the path laid out. Two people with similar backgrounds can have very different interpretations, leading to their subsequent actions creating different results, one leading to success, the other floundering, blaming the system, their territory, the franchisor, anything but themselves!

So what did I do...

Followed the model, embraced and believed in the brand and the systems. I perfected both my and my team's presentation of our service offering through continual checks with my franchisor and his support team. We took the sector-specific marketing materials, we segmented our data and posted out personalized mailshots, we followed up with emails and telephone calls and we refined our lists.

A mixture of social media and Google AdWords drove traffic to our new local website landing page where prospects could watch our personal promo video. This video introduced the key service differentiators; I spoke as a passionate franchisee and also about the local area.

We sent more emails, always personal and with relevant content. We did more telemarketing and hit the streets, knocking on doors looking to introduce ourselves, raise awareness, search out the decision-makers and understand the prospects' current situation.

The key to our success has been an integrated approach. Good collateral, a marketing activity schedule and ongoing training in perfecting the delivery of the promotional messages – those differentiators relevant to each target audience. Unlike starting without a franchise model, this was not trial and error to find out what works, it was a process of refining our understanding and application of the proven tools.

So in summary: I believe that you need to believe in the brand, believe in your offering, follow the model, but equally importantly you need to ensure you have understood the route laid out and continually check that you are implementing as intended. Enjoy every moment that you can and remember that it is very unlikely to go exactly as you thought it would!

Chris Cook, chartered marketer and franchisee, Betterclean Services

Case study: Mr Electric

In 2008 I purchased the Mr Electric franchise (resale) from the current owner, the idea being to run it alongside my fire and flood restoration franchise, with a shared office and office staff. I was sure I could get work from my contacts in the fire and flood restoration industry and my network of contacts built up over the years. This time I had cash flows, a plan, etc. It was easier since I had an idea of where the work was going to come from. It can be a waste of time going into something where you have no real idea. I had a vision and plan and was using the franchise to gain access to bigger contracts. I accepted I would have to pay fees but looked upon them as a salesman.

Always make sure that you get value for your fees. I had done my homework, I knew the company and I knew the owner who was a very good electrician but not a salesman or businessman. I was sure I could increase sales, which were £80,000/year, with two employees. Just by that last statement you can see that I had no reason to pay more than the normal franchise fee, since despite the turnover the business was not making money.

As this was my third franchise I had noticed a few things to avoid.

Trying to impress the franchisor: in all three franchises I have seen the company 'Mr Big', the franchisee who is fantastic, go under. They had fallen for the old trap: 'turnover is vanity', whereas we know profits are sanity and cash is king. One had a fantastic turnover, rookie of the year award, franchisee of the year award, and was in the final of the national franchisee of the year. Fantastic turnover and you could not beat the image he projected. No structure though: invoices being produced late, no chasing of invoices, and the quality of work wasn't great.

Another one again had fantastic turnover, far better quality, but paid out a fortune in commissions advertising and ended up in administration.

Beware: you are going into business – a franchisor can and will help you survive but success is still up to you. I was sent by Mr Electric on a leadership course where I found out that I was a pretty good leader but to get to the next level I needed to change a few things. This opened my eyes to the fact that even though I had been fairly successful, I knew nothing technically about running a business.

Franchisors often have business development managers, but in my experience they are not business coaches. They can sometimes be simply box-tickers checking up on you. You would not dream of being an electrician without training, but people just go into business thinking they can just survive. I have found that certain types of people struggle to build a decent-sized business. Control freaks, the type that say: 'I will not ask anyone to do something I can't do myself'. That's the point of staff.

People who can't trust anyone to do a job as good as they can, people who cannot relate to the feelings of others will struggle to get the best out of staff. The person who thinks leadership is shouting and bawling like a sergeant-major. These types can do well as a one-man band but will never be able to inspire a team. It is important you learn about leadership, finances, strategy, psychology; have a vision and communicate that vision. It is no good just saying our vision is to give the best customer service in the industry.

You have to praise staff for great customer service, reward them and show staff how it sets your company apart from others. **It is important you know how to handle different people.**

I am colour blind and know virtually nothing about electrics, but we will have a £1.1 million turnover this year with a good net profit. My electricians are no better than any other electricians. I have a few assets: one being that I am useless at everything. A strange asset but it means that I am happy to trust my staff and am willing for them to have input on how the job should be done. All I have is a vision of the type of service

I want to give and that aim runs through my company. If you are thinking of starting any sort of business write down the vision of just what you want that company to look like.

Periodically look at that vision and compare what you have built.

I know someone who owns a couple of lunchtime restaurants serving jacket potatoes and pork rolls. Her vision could well have been to serve first-class food quickly and politely with staff cleaning tables the moment people leave, etc. When I went in there the floor had food all over it, tables were full of the previous customers' food, and the staff were standing about while the customers were waiting to be served. She needed to revisit her vision and work towards it rather than being too involved on the shop floor. She needed to stand back and see what she had created.

What I have done is not hard but very, very few people manage it. We answer the phone, something that most tradesmen fail to achieve! We give a time slot and the electrician calls while on the way. He wears a uniform, carries ID, and puts overshoes on. We communicate with customers all the things that feature in my or your ideal way to run an electrical business. The only difference is I stick to it and instil it into our culture.

Jeff Longley, franchisee Mr Electric

Focus points

✲ Follow the model that the franchisor gives you – it's there for a reason.

✲ Remember that you should always consider the business reason behind what you are doing.

✲ While the franchisor is there to help you, success is down to you.

✲ Sometimes, business success comes down to doing the fundamentals well – making sure that you look after your staff and your customers.

Next step

In this chapter, we received some useful feedback from existing franchisees about what has worked, and what hasn't, in their business. In the next chapter we will hear from franchisors about their experiences.

18

Tips from those who've been there, seen it and done it

In this chapter you will learn:

▶ *Feedback from existing franchisors*
▶ *Why you should follow the system*
▶ *How to deal with your franchisor.*

Following on from the case studies from franchisees in the previous chapter, we now have a range of franchisors who have kindly provided their top tips in respect of running a franchise business. As with the quotes from franchisors, these have been provided as feedback for you on the areas that they wished franchisees knew about before starting a franchise.

Remember this: Advice from a franchisor

Many of us harbour the ambition to be our own boss. How much better would life be if we were free of the restrictions and bureaucracy of employment and in control of our own destiny, to be the boss making our own decisions?

Self-employment can be very liberating and rewarding, from both a financial and lifestyle viewpoint. However, it's definitely not for everyone. Many of us may have the desire to run our own business, but do we all have what it takes to go it alone and be successful? Clearly not. Lack of confidence, limited capital or simply being too risk averse are common and understandable reasons why a lot of people shy away from leaving the relative security and comfort of being employed to start their own business.

Franchising represents a great way to overcome some of the typical obstacles confronted by budding business owners because it offers the chance to run a business that's already proven, with an established brand, system and methodologies. You are trained to run the business and given on-going support. So, it's a 'fast track' route to setting up a business with the associated risks considerably reduced. That benefit is very appealing and explains why franchising has matured into being a major contributor to the UK economy.

Franchising does not, however, overcome the importance of having the right character, attitude and personality. A franchise is not a soft option for owning a business. In fact, the demands can be greater because not only are franchise owners accountable to themselves and their family about how the business performs, they are also accountable to the franchisor. The franchisor expects that franchise owners will rigorously conform with prescribed systems and methods and they will set performance standards which franchise owners will be carefully measured against.

Clive Smith, franchisor MagicMan, franchising and franchise consultant

Remember this: Advice from a franchisor

The franchisor has a successful business model. Running a successful business and keeping it successful is hard work. Understanding your weaknesses – everyone has them. In the 21st century most ethical franchisors recognize that having the right type of franchisee for their businesses saves both time and resources. This is made difficult if you are not open with your franchisor, and do not expect the franchisor to have a crystal ball. Be open with your franchisor about your business, including your figures. You should understand and know your figures at all times. Use the time with your franchisor to build your business, since the franchisor is there to help you. Provide feedback: if something is working well share it with your franchisor. A successful network will increase your ROI (return on investment) when you sell your business and exit the network.

Bev Regan, franchisor of Aspect and former franchisee

Remember this: Advice from a franchisor

I recall being interviewed when I wanted to be a franchisee in 2005. I was with my husband and, since the franchise business was something she had first-hand knowledge of, my Mum also joined us. We were like puppies. The franchisor gave us lots of information and answered every question that we asked. It was very exciting. No promises were made – but I *heard* promises. I was given a spreadsheet to complete with financial details. When I put in one extra 'job' the figures grew. It was really enticing. The problem is: I just did not look beyond that meeting. I didn't ask the right questions because I didn't really know what they were. I did not experience one moment when the franchisor tried to put me off by delivering any of the downside of being a franchisee in that business. I had not done my due diligence about being a franchisee at all...

Louise Harris, franchisor of Wilkins Chimney Sweep and former franchisee

Remember this: Advice from a franchisor

When choosing a franchise, look at yourself in the mirror and ask: 'Can I envision myself running this type of business in the medium to long term; will it excite me, will it give me the lifestyle and challenges I'm looking for?' If you answer 'yes' then do everything possible to follow your dream of self-employment with that franchise.

Ken Deary, former franchisee, and now franchisor of Right at Home

Remember this: Advice from a franchisor

The most successful franchisees are nearly always the ones who most closely follow the franchisor's system. While going 'off-piste' may result in you discovering a better way to do things, usually it just leads to frustration when you learn the hard way why that particular method wasn't in the franchisor's manual to begin with! While you're spending time re-inventing the wheel, proper operating procedures can get overlooked, which will set you back further than any gains you might have hoped to make by implementing your brilliant new idea.

That is not to say that you shouldn't suggest new ideas, however. Part of the strength of a franchise network comes from sharing the collective wisdom gleaned by the experience of all of the franchisees. The key is 'ask before you try' since you may well find that your brilliant 'new' idea was tried several years ago with disastrous consequences! A quick email or phone call to the franchisor asking: 'Is there any reason why we don't do X?' may well elicit a response of: 'Yes, we tried it and it doesn't work' or 'No, but let us test it in a controlled manner on our own (more established) business'. You don't want to be experimenting with new ideas on your brand-new – and therefore very vulnerable – business.

Steve Felmingham, franchisor Banana Moon Day Nurseries

Remember this: Advice from a franchisor

A franchise has a typical survival rate of 93 per cent, so is more likely to successfully trade beyond its first three years compared to a startup business. Hence, franchising is by far the safest way of running your own business! It offers you an out-of-the-box business opportunity where the majority of the issues have been highlighted and overcome either during the pilot stages or by earlier franchisees in the system. How many times have you heard the phrase 'been there, done that, got the t-shirt'? Well in essence that's franchising; someone else has taken the less calculated risks and has learned the lessons that they then pass on to you.

Franchisees I have worked with in the past have made many comments to me about the main benefits of franchising; however, the ones that stand out are:

✳ 'It's hard work, but at least I am doing it for myself not for a corporate concern; I am in control of my own destiny.'

✳ 'The help and support you receive from the franchisor is absolutely priceless; at the beginning when you are going through the "doubting your decision" stage, they are there to help and guide you through the darker times. They're there to help you and keep control of your business when times are lean and, moreover, they are there by your side when the good times come.'

✳ 'If you had to go out and "buy-in" the support structure a franchisor offers you, such as advertising, marketing, financial guidance, human resources, purchasing support, etc., then it would cost you a small fortune. I get the benefit of putting a small amount of cash in each month but get the benefit of a large fund for this purpose.'

✳ 'Since buying my franchise my quality of life has vastly improved. I can now chose to pick up the kids from school and all my family comment on how cheerier I am than ever I was as an employee.'

✳ 'Simply the best decision I have ever made!'

The single biggest piece of advice I can personally give any prospective franchisee is simply FOLLOW THE MODEL, read the manual from cover to cover (several times) and do as it says, it's that simple. So many franchisee businesses I have worked with, when asked 'What makes you successful?', answered... 'I follow the model!'. Conversely, the ones who aren't so successful – didn't!

Dave Galvin, franchisor Dwyer Group

Remember this: Advice from a franchisor

The importance of the business plan – following it, and reviewing it – is perhaps the key determining factor in the success of a franchise, and in fact any business! Make sure that you know where you are going, and that you constantly check your progress along the way. Also, it might sound obvious but make sure that your goals are in alignment with your business plan, both from a business perspective and personally. Sometimes people get lost in the operations of their business with the day-to-day distractions, and lose focus on what's really important.

Rob Oyston, franchisor Sports Xtra

Remember this: Advice from a franchisor

Although this might not suit every franchise, you should aim to have a business that is dependent on excellent systems rather than excellent people, as there is a risk that excellent people can be run over by a bus! Also, when it comes to resale, you can't have a business that is dependent on you. At its simplest, the franchise should provide you with both an ongoing income and a resale value – both of these will be increased if you can build it as a business rather than as a job.

Simon Mills, franchisor Seriously FUN Swimming Schools

Remember this: Advice from a franchisor

Be brave and be bold, but keep your eyes open and choose a franchise that plays to your strengths and interests but also appeals to your own values. A proven system can massively reduce the risk of starting your own business, but the success of that venture will always lie in your own hard work and adherence to the model.

Suzie McCafferty, former franchisor Platinum Wave

Remember this: Advice from a franchisor

Buying a franchise does not guarantee success; you have to work just as hard to set up your exclusive territory. Sitting back and expecting it to grow by itself doesn't work.

Keep a good amount of working capital in your projections: like any new business, profits can take a while to appear. Make sure you don't stretch yourself thinly and therefore end up putting undue pressure on yourself and your business.

Communicate! If you're doing well, shout about it and if you're struggling ask for help. The reason you bought a franchise was for the invaluable support you receive from not only head office but the other franchisees in your network. Share, talk, email and keep communicating. This keeps you motivated and constantly reminds you why you bought into the business.

Enjoy it! By choosing a franchise you have a passion for it. It should be a good type of hard work! There are so many different types of franchise opportunities out there to choose from so make the right choice for you.

Anne-Marie Martin, franchisor Diddi Dance

Focus points

✱ Franchising is not an easy option – not only are you accountable to yourself and your family, you are also accountable to your franchisor, who will have certain performance expectations.

✱ Always be open with your franchisor, both about the problems in your franchise but also don't be afraid to share your success stories.

✱ Make sure that you follow the system. It has been developed based on the experiences of your franchisor and your fellow franchisees.

✱ Keep track of your business performance against your original business plan. Things can and will change along the way, but this review process can make sure that you stay on track.

Next step

We have now heard feedback from both franchisees and franchisors about the advice that they would give to those just coming into the franchising world. In the next chapter, we will look at the support that you should receive from your franchisor.

Part Six

Running a franchise

19

What support should you expect from the franchisor?

In this chapter you will learn:

▶ *What your franchisor should be offering you*

▶ *What the operations manual is*

▶ *The types of meeting that franchisors provide.*

As mentioned earlier in the book, the main difference between a franchise investment and starting your own independent business is the level of support that you can expect from head office.

In my experience, head offices come in different shapes and sizes, depending on the size of the franchise network, the complexity of their franchisees' businesses, the level of support that they want to give you, and how 'corporate' the head office business is.

As a general rule of thumb, a startup network with fewer than 15 franchisees will generally be operated and managed by the founder; however, by the time that they have reached 20 franchisees they are often stretched and looking to employ a franchise manager! A 'corporate' network owned by a listed PLC will have an entirely different setup to an independent network in that there will be a pre-defined management and reporting structure; placing additional staffing demand on the head office.

When a network is growing, it will tend to employ regional managers to help manage the franchisees. Typically, a franchise manager will look to both support you and also ensure that you are complying with the operations manual and the franchise agreement. As this person will be your main contact at head office, it is worth trying to meet before committing to the franchise, so that you can be sure that you can work with the franchise manager.

Key idea: Advice from an expert

Your franchisor's job is to recruit, train, monitor and motivate people who want to run their own business. Their support should therefore range across the entire spectrum of initially making sure you and their business are right for each other, then ensuring that you both get the best from operating the system in question. That includes, when the time comes, helping you to exit from the business by finding or approving someone to buy your business from you.

The sort of support that franchisees like is where the franchisor comes up with branding and marketing ideas, maybe even helping with securing sales, and is also active in research and development so that new products or processes can be introduced once they have been proven to work. They may also deal with any legislative requirements or administration procedures that would otherwise be a time-consuming distraction for an individual operator. Outsourcing the mundane aspects of the business to trusted suppliers is also a bonus.

The sort of support franchisees don't like is being made to toe the line or 'follow the system', which is an essential function if both parties are to succeed. 'That's fine for all the other franchisees, but I don't need it!'

In my experience the best support a franchisor can provide is helping you to 'run the business' not just 'run the outlet'. Initially agreeing a business plan then regularly reviewing and adapting it, based on some key performance indicators that are used across the network, is essential. This may include training you in financial awareness, such as understanding the differences between turnover, profit and cash, but will ideally also provide you with coaching or mentoring services since 'being part of something' is the reason most franchisees become franchisees rather than going it alone.

Brian Duckett, The Franchising Centre

Practical help from your franchisor

So, practically, what kind of things would a typical franchisor do for you? Below is a list of some of the things that I've seen in different networks. Please bear in mind that this list isn't exhaustive, nor does it mean that a franchisor that doesn't offer each and every service is underperforming! Therefore, this is best used as a general guide to the range of services and support that you can expect from a franchisor.

TRAINING

▶ Provide you with initial training on how to 'do the job' or 'sell the goods'

▶ Provide you with initial training on how to run a business, including:

     ▷ Marketing training

     ▷ Sales training

     ▷ Financial training

     ▷ Administration training

▶ Provide you with ongoing training on new developments and regulatory updates

▶ Provide you with soft skills, personal development and management training

▶ Provide you with training to help you convert your business to a saleable asset.

MARKETING

▶ Provide you with a marketing plan for the year ahead

▶ Support you with your initial launch

▶ Provide you with brand guidelines and templated documents

▶ Provide you with a template website

▶ Manage the national content on your website

▶ Provide you with a social media template and manual

▶ Provide you with content for your social media accounts

▶ Automate the content distribution on your social media accounts

▶ Provide you with template press releases for local distribution

▶ Provide you with an outsourced marketing agency for local implementation

▶ Provide you with an online resource for ordering pre-designed marketing material.

BUSINESS ADMINISTRATION

▶ Offer a CRM system for you to manage your customer database

▶ Offer an EPOS system to manage the administration of your sales receipts

▶ Offer a timetable/diary system to manage your time

▶ Offer a quotation and invoicing system to make sure that you have the highest chance of being paid

▶ Provide you with an accounting system to ensure compliance to HMRC regulations and the operations manual

▶ Provide you with a document management system to streamline your workflows

▶ Provide you with a sales ledger, or full accounting service, to handle your bookkeeping and accountancy compliance

▶ Provide you with a list of approved suppliers

▶ Support with staff contracts and employment legislation

▶ Support with Health & Safety and other business legislation.

BUSINESS IMPROVEMENT

▶ Regularly check your actual business performance back to your business and operational plan

▶ Compare your marketing activity to your ROI (return on investment)

▶ Compare your business performance to the rest of the network through benchmarking

▶ Compare your operational performance and activities to the rest of the network

▶ Identify new products and services that you can offer through the franchise

▶ Identify new marketing activities that you can undertake

▶ Provide hands-on support during difficult times

▶ Provide advice and assistance based on their experience of dealing with many other franchisees.

PRODUCT DEVELOPMENT

► Identify current and future trends in your industry

► Perform national market research

► Identify upsell opportunities for their franchisees

► Identify new markets, products and services for the entire network

► Ensure that any future threats are identified and avoided early on.

NATIONAL INFLUENCE

► Provide you with product suppliers who can offer you preferential terms

► Provide you with business advisers such as accountants and insurance brokers who know your franchise and can offer preferential terms

► Influence within any trade associations that exist for your industry

► Influence within the national press

► Influence with politicians.

Key idea: Advice from an expert

A successful network is run by a franchisor who understands that developing and supporting franchisees, in an environment that enables them to make money, is crucial.

Damian Humphrey, Ashton KCJ

Operations manual

A major document that underpins the franchise is the operations manual. While this might conjure up an image of a dusty old book that gets unwrapped and put into a drawer, in today's world these are quite likely to be delivered online. Regardless of format, it's important that both franchisee and franchisor see the operations manual as a 'loose leaf binder' rather than as a hardback bound book: it should grow and change organically as the business and the wider world changes.

The operations manual has no defined form, and therefore could be as long or as short as the concept requires. What is consistent is that the manual should be comprehensive in covering both the way to do the job and the way to run the business. You would expect the manual to include the ground rules of the business – including brand guidelines, operational obligations, administrative obligations, and financial and operational reporting requirements.

Remember this: Advice from a franchisor

As most franchisors will tell you, the operations manual is a bible! It is what everything else hinges on and is probably the most important document any franchise has.

It's imperative that operations are standardized and structured. This is something that gets increasingly important as the network grows. Customers want the same level of service from every branch, shop or restaurant. It gives the franchisee the autonomy to make operational decisions and the confidence to grow the business without constantly checking in with the franchisor.

They need to be comprehensive so that guesswork is minimized. The more concise and detailed the manual is, the more the business will be protected and the less likely it is that mistakes will be made.

Manuals are always on the large side. They have to be! They are constantly being updated as the network grows and end up at least twice their original size.

It doesn't have to be a 'manual' in the traditional sense. Some franchisors prefer to offer bite-size chunks of training and information. Most importantly, it needs to be in plain English so franchisees will actually want to read it!

Jo Tomlinson, franchisor We Love Pets

SO, WHAT IS THE IMPORTANCE OF THE MANUAL?

I have to be honest, in writing this book I received a case study from a franchisee (who shall remain anonymous) jokingly referring to the operations manual as being great for wedging the door open. While this might be a cynical view, it's important that both franchisor and franchisee understand the huge benefit that the manual can bring. Without wanting to labour the point, a key benefit of buying a franchise is that you are buying a proven blueprint for running a successful business. That blueprint is contained within the manual!

From a franchisor's perspective, there's a vested interest in you being successful; but also just as strong an interest in making sure that the network is providing a consistent brand and process experience to each and every person who comes into contact with the franchise. Therefore, franchisors will make sure that you are complying with the manual, either through informal franchise management or operational audits.

Remember this: Advice from a franchisor

Always remember that a franchise is not a guarantee of an easy life – it is a proven system, but you will still have to drive the business and follow the franchisor's system to the letter. This takes energy and commitment – perhaps a little less than starting a non-franchised business, but not much. The difference is that you don't have to learn by trial and error – because someone's already done that for you.

Partway through the journey you will inevitably lose sight of this; your franchisor is nagging you about using the wrong typeface on your leaflets; two of your staff have left just because you hadn't got around to giving them a proper contract and one of your customers has had the cheek to complain about you to head office. The world is against you, and you are feeling disheartened.

First, remind yourself that every franchisee has gone through those feelings of despondency at some point. Sit down with your franchisor and explain how you feel, but be prepared to be shown where you have drifted away from the system. In most successful businesses, detail really matters. You wouldn't see a marketing communication from Virgin Media using the wrong shade of red would you? For your franchise to be a success you will

Franchisor meetings and conferences

As part of a franchise, one of the biggest benefits that you will receive is access to the regional meetings and annual conferences that most franchisors run. As with most areas of support, every franchise is different, and the extent of these meetings depends on the size of your network and the way that things are done in that network.

The thing that most franchise networks offer, regardless of shape or size, is an annual conference. This is often used by franchisors as an opportunity to update franchisees about relevant changes to the market and the operations. Many networks allow accredited suppliers to exhibit at their conferences, or provide specialist seminars for the franchisees. There is often a motivational side to these events as well, with a range of awards offered to both new and existing franchisees.

In my experience, when a franchise network has a reasonable level of coverage, it looks to supplement its annual conference with regional meetings. This allows a more regular contact between the head office team and the franchisees, and gives the franchisor a chance to understand what is going on at ground level. It goes without saying that the regional meetings are, by their very nature, smaller meetings than the annual conferences, due to the smaller catchment areas.

From the events that I've been invited to, I've noticed a difference between the tone of these two types of meeting. Generally, the regional meetings will be a 'meeting' style arrangement, with perhaps a roundtable, and a more formal agenda with participation expected from all attendees. Conversely, the annual conferences are more of an event, with theatre/cabaret-style seating, and guest speakers will provide the content for the conference. Sometimes, there are breakout sessions, where franchisees can choose which subjects they wish to learn more about. There is also a significant social element to most conferences, with the dinner and awards presentations giving franchisees a chance to get to know each other and share best practice.

Focus points

* Franchise networks come in all shapes and sizes, depending on the complexity of the model, the number of franchisees, and how corporate the head office is.
* Support is often a double-edged sword – while some support is viewed positively by franchisees, there is also a level of support that is to help ensure conformity to the system.
* Franchisors offer a range of support services, covering a huge variety of areas. There is no 'one size fits all' and every network is different.
* It is important to look past the glossy brochure and sales prospectus, and look for evidence of the support provided and how it is delivered.
* The operations manual will provide you with the 'how', to help you run the business. Your agreement will require you to operate in line with this manual.
* There are various types of meetings hosted by franchisors. Take advantage of them, and use the opportunities to meet fellow franchisees and approved suppliers.

Next step

In this chapter we've looked at the importance of the operations manual and the support that head office should provide you with. In the next chapter we will touch on the basics of managing your business finances.

Managing your finances

In this chapter you will learn:

▶ *The basics of managing your franchise finances*
▶ *What a set of financial reports looks like*
▶ *Some top tips to help your cash flow.*

One of the key tasks of a new franchise owner is making sure that finances are well managed. Often, a new franchise is run on a minimal budget, and as such effective cash flow management is key. You don't need to be an accountant to manage your cash position, but you do need to be aware of some key statistics within your business to ensure that a downward trend doesn't leave you with more month remaining than money!

There is an often repeated phrase in business, which you might have heard before:

> *Turnover is Vanity*
>
> *Profit is Sanity*
>
> *but Cash is King*

This saying highlights a key area that some new business owners forget: ultimately, your staff, suppliers, landlord, and your franchisor will need paying, and cash is vital for the health of a business.

One of the first areas that new franchisees get confused on when it comes to financial matters is the difference between cashflow and profit. Did you know that a business could have £150,000 profit on paper, but be overdrawn with its bank and be struggling with cash flow? Once you have an understanding of the differences, it is obvious; however, many business owners don't immediately understand this financial area.

There are various items that may be included within a profit & loss account that may not be directly reflected in your bank account. If you make a trade sale to another business, it would often have payment terms attached, and as such you might have to wait 30 days (or more) to get paid. Similarly, you would have payment terms on your purchases once you are an established business, and again your bank account wouldn't reflect these expenses until the payment is made.

Keeping track of the figures

It's vital that you get a grasp on your banking position, and make sure that this is reconciled to your original cash flow projections that you have prepared in your business plan. This will allow you to identify at an early stage any trends that need addressing, and will also help you make sure that you are on track. Projections are at best educated guesswork, and as such it could very well be the case that you have budgeted incorrectly. The only way that you will know this is by keeping track of your finances to ensure that you are reasonably close to, or performing better than, expected.

There are numerous ways to manage a franchise business's finances, such as:

MANUAL BOOKKEEPING

It is possible to satisfy HM Revenue & Customs by simply maintaining a cashbook of your income and expenditure periodically. This has become far less common over the past few years, as adoption of computerized systems has increased. The main issue with managing your finances in this way is that reporting is very time consuming, and there is a large risk of arithmetical errors. You will also need to employ an accountant who is happy to work with manual records so that you can file your tax returns; and even if you find one that is, it's unlikely that your franchisor would be happy with this method of bookkeeping.

EXCEL SPREADSHEETS

Many businesses that once used manual cashbooks have replicated these systems onto a spreadsheet. Although this allows you to put in formulae to add up columns and rows, it is far more difficult to report on the figures using Excel, particularly if you are not proficient with spreadsheet usage.

DESKTOP SOFTWARE

I've used the term 'desktop' to denote any software package that is installed onto a PC or Mac, such as Sage or QuickBooks. Typically, these packages cost between £100 and £500, and are available as an online download or at any software retailer. They allow you to keep a full record of your banking activity, your sales ledger, and your purchase ledger; and also allow you to raise invoices and track any stock that you may hold.

These packages also give you a range of reporting functions, such as actual performance vs budget, profit & loss accounts, balance sheets and detailed reports of creditors/debtors. These packages are now becoming outdated with the increasing adoption of cloud-based accounting software.

ONLINE SOFTWARE

Recently, there has been a shift towards online accounting, with packages such as Xero and QuickBooks Online taking the early lead in this market. They are offered as a monthly subscription, typically £10-£30, and provide you with access to your financial information on any computer, anywhere in the world. These packages allow you to use your time more effectively, as you do not need to be chained to a desk to process your bookkeeping, and often integrate with other packages such as CRM systems so that you can minimize your time spent bookkeeping. These packages can also allow you to use a 'bank feed', meaning that your banking transactions are automatically imported into the software. It seems apparent that most desktop packages are migrating to an online platform, and as such this is the route that I suggest for most franchisees.

Financial training

You might find that your franchisor dictates which package you should use for your franchise, as often they would look to consolidate their franchisees' financial performance for benchmarking purposes. If, however, you have the choice, once you have identified one or two packages that you feel may be suitable for your business, you should then decide how best to purchase the software and how to get trained on it. Most accountants and bookkeepers get discounted versions of software by being members of partner programmes offered by the software houses. So it's worth negotiating to see if you can get a discount passed on by them, or instead whether they can bundle the licence cost into their fees if it will save them time.

Training is a particular issue that I see with many independent businesses, and often a relatively low amount of time spent in the early days will save you significant accountancy bills should your records not be accurate and reconciled. Your franchisor should handle some level of financial training; however, if not you will need to investigate training options independently.

Again, do some research about both generic bookkeeping courses, and one-to-one training (often provided by accountants) to see what works best for you. Usually, I find that the best programme of training includes an initial training session with actual data, perhaps one month into trading, together with a follow-up session two months later to ensure that you are on track with your bookkeeping. This way, you can get an 'all clear' from your accountant, and then ensure that there should be no additional costs when it comes to the year-end.

Financial reports

The types of reports that you would expect to understand are the following:

PROFIT & LOSS ACCOUNT

This report details all income and expenditure in the business from an accounting perspective. Therefore, it doesn't include capital expenses, such as the cost of fixed assets, or your original investment. This report is usually prepared for a period of time, such as a specific month or a financial year, and it will show the net profit of your business at the bottom of the page (hence why it is referred to colloquially as the 'bottom line').

There are various 'key performance indicators' that you should monitor within your profit & loss account, such as:

► **Turnover** – this is the value of sales (before VAT) during the period.

► **Gross profit %** – this is the profit that you make after deducting 'direct costs' (costs attributable directly to sales, such as product purchases). It is this percentage that you should monitor carefully if you sell products or have any other costs closely tied to your sales, since a small change in the percentage can lead to a large change in your net profit.

▶ **Overheads** – these are displayed in the profit & loss account below the gross profit. Each business has different overheads that require monitoring.

▶ **Net profit** – ultimately, this is the amount that the business is making, and your tax bill and the end company valuation will depend on the profitability of the business.

These KPIs are the immediately obvious items that you need to monitor; however, it is also important to acknowledge the KPIs that affect these financial results. For example, if your business depends on telesales, then the number of calls made, and the conversion rates achieved, will directly affect the turnover, and in turn the net profit.

BALANCE SHEET

This report shows a snapshot of the value of the business, based on what it owns (assets) versus what it owes (liabilities). Very simply, this report gives you a 'net worth', which would be the valuation of the business should you decide to close the business and sell all the assets for what they are worth, and repay all the loans and creditors at this specific point.

The balance sheet is made up of several components, including:

▶ **Fixed assets** – these are the assets that the business owns, and broadly speaking the assets held for more than one year (otherwise known as 'capital assets'). These can be split between 'tangible assets', which are assets that you can see and touch (for example, motor vehicles, furniture, computers and machinery); and 'intangible assets', such as licences and goodwill.

▶ **Current assets** – these are assets that are expected to be used within the day-to-day trading of the business. Items included within the current assets section are cash at bank, petty cash, debtors, and work in progress. There is usually an adjustment for 'prepayments', which is an accounting adjustment to ensure that the financial results reported are in line with what actually happened during the year, rather than based on cash flows (see below – Matching concept).

▶ **Current liabilities** – these are monies owed to other people and businesses that are of a short-term nature (less than one year), or are repayable on demand. Such liabilities include bank overdrafts, credit card liabilities, trade creditors and accruals (again, see below – Matching concept).

▶ **Long-term liabilities** – these are liabilities that have a longer term of repayment, and hence are separated from the more immediate items. These are usually more structured, and might well be secured against an asset of the company.

The above items will give a resulting balance (total assets *less* total liabilities), which is the net worth of the company, making up the first half of the balance sheet. The intention of any balance sheet is to actually balance – so there is a second half that shows how the net worth is financed (through items such as share capital and retained profit).

Balance sheets are of particular interest to financial institutions as they show the financial health of the business, and allow the reader to determine whether the business has enough 'liquid assets' (current assets *less* current liabilities) to continue trading.

A key difference that you need to bear in mind when comparing the balance sheet to the profit & loss account is that the balance sheet is simply a 'snapshot' of the business at a single point in time, whereas the profit & loss account is a report on the performance of the business over a period of time.

MATCHING (ACCRUALS) CONCEPT

You will have seen reference to items such as accruals and prepayments within the description of accounting reports. The reason that these adjustments have to take place is that there is an accounting principle of matching, which dictates that accounting reports have to reflect the actual nature of the transactions for the year.

For example, at the end of the year a business might have incurred costs with a supplier that were not invoiced until a month after the period end. According to the matching concept, these costs should be reported against the period (and, in turn, the income) to which they relate.

This can also work the other way around – a supplier might invoice in advance of actually providing their service or product, so, in turn, the financial reports should be adjusted to reflect this.

These adjustments are commonly known as 'cut-off' adjustments, as they do not change the value of income or expenses, merely the period in which they are reported. For most small businesses these adjustments affect the overheads section of the profit & loss account (for items such as insurance and accountancy fees); however, for some businesses these adjustments affect their gross profit margin, and as such should be monitored regularly to ensure that they are accurate, and in turn that the gross profit margin is being accurately managed.

Managing your cash flow

Fundamentally, the reason why most businesses fail comes down to a cash flow problem – whether it is another business failure that leaves them with a bad debt, a change in market conditions that they can't adapt to quickly enough, or simply their funding being withdrawn – a problem with cash flow can very quickly lead to a business having to close its doors.

Because of this risk, it is vital that all businesses take every step possible to ensure that their cash flow is managed effectively. Here are some tips that might seem simple, but will ensure that you manage your finances effectively to maximize your chance of success.

▶ **Invoice your customers promptly** – If you do not raise your invoices promptly, you have little chance of getting paid promptly! I have a little rule that I like to apply personally, which is that the value of any work done for a customer goes down for each day that you delay invoicing. What I mean by this is that customers are most enthusiastic about the service or product you provide on the day of purchase. If you then wait two months to invoice them for it, the initial feelings are likely to have disappeared.

▶ **Make sure you invoice everything you can** – Again, this is another obvious tip. However, it surprises me how many businesses I see (in all industries) that do not have a system to ensure that all work done, or all products sold, are actually invoiced. This is perhaps more vital than the first tip – as although a late invoice may get paid, an invoice that is never raised is never paid!

▶ **Make sure you invoice accurately** – While it is important to ensure that you invoice everything you can, it is also wise not to invoice any more than what you should. Not only is this practice unethical and illegal if done deliberately, it will also give the customer an opportunity to dispute the invoice, which will drag out the length of time before you get payment from them. Therefore, it is vital that you ensure that you have an accurate invoicing system that can help you avoid errors on invoices.

▶ **Set appropriate due dates** – Many businesses seem to default to 30-day terms of payment; however, I often find that businesses of all types adopt these terms with little consideration of the terms that they would like to set. While certain large customers require you to fit in with their payment policies, it is up to you to determine what your terms of business are. Also, make sure that your accounting system can handle the terms of business that you require, since some software packages can only handle fixed terms of 30 days.

▶ **Chase your debts** – Once you have raised an invoice, and set a due date, it is important to actually chase the debt! Provided that your system can report on it, make sure that you have a regular report of debtors, and have a fixed follow-up process to contact your customers. The best processes tend to include courtesy calls to ensure that the invoices have been received before they are due, a reminder on the due date, if not paid by then, followed by a series of escalating letters that ultimately end in a letter before action should you need to take further recovery action. There are several debt collection agencies who can help you at this stage, and often the introduction of a third party is all you need to get payment from your late-paying customers. Many business owners get worried about chasing debts, due to a fear of upsetting their customers. Keep in mind that a customer who doesn't pay you is usually not worth keeping as a customer!

▶ **Use free-of-charge credit from your suppliers** – Having extolled the virtues of effective credit control, it is worth remembering that in turn your suppliers will have payment terms, and you are able to use these to your advantage. If a supplier gives you 30 days' credit, try to use this credit as part of the overall funding of your business. I am not suggesting that you perpetually pay late, but do make sure that you take advantage of the permitted credit terms. It is, however, worthwhile reviewing your suppliers' terms of business to see if there are any opportunities for early settlement discounts, and indeed consider whether it is worth using these yourself on your own invoices.

▶ **Monitor your bank account regularly** – With online banking there is no excuse for not knowing exactly where your financial position is on every single day. Make sure that you also have a projection of how the upcoming days, weeks and months look, even if only a rough calculation, so that you can take action to improve your cash flow position earlier rather than later.

▶ **Keep your financiers up to date** – If you do happen to anticipate cash flow difficulties, make sure that you speak to your bankers as early as possible since they may be able to support you through any difficult times. Your bank has a vested interest in allowing you to continue trading, and provided that you approach them intelligently with a sensible proposal, they would be likely to want to help you through any rough periods with additional facilities. It's important to avoid burying your head in the sand on these matters, as financial support is very difficult to obtain (and usually expensive!) after the event.

▶ **Keep your franchisor up to date** – Again, if you anticipate cash flow difficulties, make sure that you speak to your franchisor as early as possible. Many franchisees are afraid of sharing problems with their franchisor, either through embarrassment or a misplaced fear that the franchisor will look to terminate their agreement. In reality, the franchisor has a vested interest in ensuring that your business is successful, since a profitable and successful network is the best possible sales tool for them when recruiting new franchisees. Experienced franchisors would also have dealt with most business issues before, either in their own business or alongside one of their franchisees. So calling on their support sooner rather than later is one of the benefits that you are paying for!

▶ **Stay on top of your tax** – This might seem obvious, but it is vital to make sure that you have sufficient provision for both your personal and corporate taxes.

Focus points

* Your franchisor may dictate a certain financial management system. Usually this is to help you, since they can benchmark your performance against other franchisees.

* A franchisor has a vested interest in you being profitable because a successful network grows from successful franchisees. Ask your franchisor how you can improve your profit, not just your turnover.

* Your franchisor may insist that you prepare your accounts in a certain way. Again, this is to help you – the information is needed in a consistent format so that relevant feedback can be provided.

* The old saying of 'Cash is King' is one of the most important phrases in business. Know your cash position, know tomorrow's cash position, and always make sure that you are on top of your invoicing and cash collection.

Next step

In this chapter we looked at some of the theory behind managing your business finances, and some practical tips to help you manage your cash flow. In particular we saw that there are certain things that a franchisor might enforce, for good reason. In the next chapter we will look at how you can promote your franchise.

21

Promoting your business

In this chapter you will learn:

▶ *Some of the marketing channels available to you*

▶ *How to produce a basic marketing plan*

▶ *The golden rules of local marketing.*

You will have seen from previous chapters that my fellow franchising colleagues and I all agree that a key skill required of any franchisee is the ability to promote his or her business, since purchasing a franchise is no guarantee of sales from day one.

As with pretty much everything else in relation to running a franchise, the level of support that you will receive varies depending on what your franchisor offers you as part of the package. Also, your marketing needs will vary depending on the type of business that you are running.

Some of the activities that you will need to think about are as follows:

WEBSITE

Does your franchise require a website? You might be provided with a website as part of your joining package with the franchisor; however, some networks do still leave their franchisees to create the content and are only involved in this process to ensure that it fits with the brand guidelines. In general, however, you should expect your franchisor to provide this for you.

SOCIAL MEDIA

Does your franchisor automate your social media presence, or are you expected to manage this yourself? Your franchisor should at least provide you with some social media guidelines, which will set out what you should and shouldn't do on social media; and a suggested approach on how to set up your profiles. It is also worth speaking to the franchisor to ensure that you are represented on the social media networks that are relevant to your franchise – some businesses would benefit from visual sites such as Instagram, whereas others benefit more from professional sites like LinkedIn.

FACE-TO-FACE NETWORKING

Something that your franchisor cannot do for you is the face-to-face networking that is often required in your local area. Make sure that you look into the groups that are operating in your region, and get yourself registered with a few different networks so that you can find one that works for you. Some networks are very formalized and have a rigid structure to their meetings, and others are very relaxed. You will only know what works for you by trying the different types of meeting that are out there.

PRINTED MATERIAL

Although many communications are now online, there is almost always a need for printed material, whether this is simply a stock of letterheads, or a more comprehensive range of brochures, booklets and promotional flyers. Your franchisor should at the very least have an accredited supplier who can help you manage your printing requirements and can help ensure brand consistency. Some networks have online procurement systems that automate this side of the business for you.

PRESS RELATIONSHIPS

An oft-overlooked area of promotion is the local press. While you can pay for advertisements in almost every publication, you will also find that local press outlets are interested in local stories. Be sure to build a relationship with the local editors, and ask your franchisor whether any assistance in this area is provided.

Key idea: Advice from an expert

Marketing from day one is too late!

In terms of marketing for your new franchise, your 'first day' actually starts weeks in advance. Plan for a month of marketing activity at the very least before you officially launch to really set your business off with a bang!

It sounds quite daunting but it really needn't be. With a little planning and some creative thinking you can produce a simple but highly effective marketing plan focused on generating interest and excitement in your local area.

Marketing fact: people need to see you or your brand between 7 and 14 times before they engage with you.

When you think about that, you should start to realize that you're going to need a presence in more than one place, with a consistent message and regularly updated content. There's no golden goose or silver bullet when it comes to marketing; a combination of activities is required. Little and often is the key to success.

Utilizing your marketing tools

As part of your franchise package, you'll undoubtedly receive marketing training and a marketing collateral pack to use for promotion in your area of business. Make sure you understand what is available to you to use and then create a plan for doing so.

Your marketing plan

This can be produced on a simple Excel spreadsheet. Use a tab for each month and list all the activities you're going to undertake, how often and a target for each. For example:

Activity	When	Target	Actual	Leads
Leaflet drops	Every Tuesday at 10am	20/day		
Prospect telephone calls	Every day at 2pm	5/day		
Update website	1 new article per month	1		

Have a column for actuals so that you can monitor yourself against your targets. If you're falling behind you need to ask yourself why and take steps to rectify the situation. By adding a column for any leads received as a result of the various activities each month, you can start to build a picture of what works best for you. Review your ongoing activity to focus on the more successful areas for maximum results.

Working with the media

Don't be afraid of the media and don't think that being in a magazine means you have to pay for it. Building a good relationship with local journalists and editors of publications is a brilliant way to boost coverage for your business.

In the months leading up to launch, research all the relevant newspapers and magazines in your area and get in touch. Explain who you are, what you're doing and see how you can add value by telling your story, contributing opinion as a local business owner or even offering expert advice for regular features. This type of PR is ideal for building trust and setting you as the expert in your field.

Collate all your research into a media list so you know who writes for what publication, what topics they like to write about and how to contact them. Try to write at least one article a month to send out. This should be non-salesy and informative to get the best chance of being published.

Networking

There's no stronger lead than a referral. Attending networking events in your local area and meeting other small business owners can be a great way to build up a referral pipeline. Normally early in the morning, these events kick off with a 'show and tell' giving you the opportunity to explain your business and what you can offer. After that it's about sharing best practice and being part of the scene. Be careful not to get too bogged down by trying to attend too many!

Social presence

Twitter, LinkedIn, Facebook and Google+ are just a few platforms that you'll need to consider utilizing for a well-rounded social presence. Decide what's going to be right for you depending on whether you're B2B or B2C (it doesn't have to be them all!) and stick to it. Make sure whatever you choose forms part of your marketing plan activity; there's nothing worse than seeing a branded social media channel that hasn't been updated for months. Get started well in advance since it takes time to build traction. Use for pushing out useful, informative messages. Have fun with it, run competitions, and show a little personality.

Be aware: social media is not a place for sales. It is a place to build relationships and interact with prospects and customers.

Golden rules for local marketing

❉ Understand the marketing tools you have available
❉ Create a simple, realistic activity plan and stick to it
❉ PR and media coverage doesn't mean paying for adverts
❉ Get to know local journalists and tell them what you're all about
❉ Create regular content for your website and press releases
❉ Be social and visible: social media matters.

As with all aspects of franchising, you're never alone, so if you need help with any of this speak to your franchisor for support but, ultimately, the more effort you put in up-front, the more you'll reap the rewards down the line.

Lucy Maisey, director Rev PR

Focus points

- A franchise generally has no guarantee of sales from day one, so your own local promotion is vital.
- Make sure you consider all available marketing channels, from 'door knocking' through to online marketing.
- A marketing plan can be as simple as an Excel spreadsheet, detailing the activity that you should do.
- Make sure that you track actual activity against target activity, as this will help you identify where things may be slipping.
- Your franchisor will have experience in dealing with franchisees' marketing plans, so make sure you get their input into these plans as well.
- The more you put into promotion and marketing, the more you will get out.

Next step

We've looked at some theory behind a franchise's finances and a franchise's promotional activities. In the next chapter we will look at an area that will probably be new to you – franchise councils.

Part Seven

Finding support

Franchise councils

In this chapter you will learn:

▶ *What a franchise council is*
▶ *How they are created*
▶ *The benefits that they bring to franchisor and franchisee.*

A feature of some very successful franchises that I work with is that they actively look to take feedback from their franchisees to help develop their business. They also act as a great opportunity for franchisors to hear the views of their network, and understand what is happening at ground level. I've asked my colleagues Suzie and Freddie to provide you with more detail about what franchise councils are, and to give you a case study about the benefits of them.

This is a guest chapter from Suzie McCafferty of Platinum Wave, with a case study from Freddie St George of Raring2go!

Key idea: Advice from an expert

Franchise councils (often referred to as franchise advisory councils or franchise exchange councils), exist to represent the views of the franchisees within a network. Structured appropriately, they can be a wonderful platform to develop new ideas, exchange best practice and bring together a group of people with much in common but who often have little opportunity to talk.

At worst, if structured inappropriately, they can be hijacked by negativity and create an 'us against them culture' in a once happy and prosperous network.

I would say all good franchisors should always have a franchise advisory council as part of their franchisee engagement strategy (although I tend to think this title is a little serious and always advise franchisors to come up with a more inclusive title for their own franchise advisory council that more accurately reflects their company values and culture).

A franchisee advisory council is a great way to learn about the needs of your network, work on progressive projects together, keep ahead of competitors and build stronger communication and engagement with your franchisees.

So let's look at how they work.

Of course, there is nothing that dictates how a franchise advisory council is set up, there are no standardized rules across the industry, so there are many different ways it can be structured.

Elections

It's easy to assume that the most democratic process is always the best way to go, but if a network is either small and new or very large and established, many of the franchisees won't know each other very well, if at all; certainly not well enough to vote on each other's suitability to represent the group. Some will feel they have to vote for the most popular and others will feel too intimidated to stand. It is good to rotate members annually, but some franchisees will undoubtedly shine in the role and both the franchisor and network will want to see them reinstated. Fairness and the pursuit of broad representation are usually the deciding factors.

Often, the franchisor will invite franchisees to join the council. It will come as no surprise that these are usually the best performing and most positive members of the network; however, it is also fair to reason that they will be the most engaged members of the group, happy to work for everyone positively rather than use the time to air personal grievances and resist progress and may also have a particular skill to contribute to the group such as a marketing, HR, sales or technology background. I didn't say this was going to be easy!

Size and balance

In an ideal world a council will have a healthy mix of men and women, new and established, some from smaller franchises and some from the larger franchises. In fact, sticking with that ideal world, you would probably say that every franchisee should be on the franchise advisory council and have their views heard and opinions consulted. In reality, however, this isn't always feasible and securing a reasonable cross-section would be a resounding success. Wherever possible, franchisors should always encourage regional representation from across the franchise network.

Friend or foe

A franchisor might think by filling the franchise advisory council with his or her strongest advocates they will have a much easier time introducing new initiatives and be subjected to fewer objections; however, franchisors have a duty to all of their franchisees and deliberately cutting out the less-loyal voices can be a recipe for disaster. Deliberately divisive figures do not a good council member make! and I think we would all agree with that.

Franchisees/franchise team

It's a difficult decision for the franchisor because all franchisors should want key members of their management team to participate and of course foster strong relationships with the rest of the group, but I think the franchisees should probably have a majority ratio of at least 3:1.

What to discuss

A common frustration among franchisee members is that the franchisor will often be looking for a new programme or initiative to simply be rubber stamped as opposed to inviting open discussion. Often this is just down to how the topic is presented. It is important to remember, though, that franchisees are investing in a franchise system that is devised and owned by the franchisor and not everything is up for negotiation and a vote.

Certainly anything that will have a direct impact on how the franchisee will be expected to manage their business, or that will create a major change, should at the very least be well presented and reasoned. The franchisees should equally feel comfortable in bringing forward any concerns among the wider group and have those issues taken seriously and addressed. I always recommend that an agenda is circulated prior to each meeting that typically includes a couple of topics that have been suggested by the franchisor and then franchisees on the franchise advisory council are then asked to put forward another couple of topics for discussion. Topics usually include new products, pricing, reporting, marketing strategy, software development and branding.

Regularity

This will hugely depend on the nature of the business and how established it is. Most franchises will try to have an annual meeting involving the entire network and perhaps a bi-annual franchise advisory council meeting that perhaps convenes around regional network meetings. Remember, franchisees will not want to have too many days away from the day-to-day management of their own operation, and nor will the franchisor want to cause any unnecessary disruption.

Formal or informal?

Meetings generally reflect the style of the management team. Regardless of whether it's suits and ties or jeans and t-shirts, the meetings should really be conducted with a formal agenda and have a chairperson and someone taking minutes to keep things in order. Without this, a well-intentioned, representative group can easily become an inefficient closed shop devoid of focus concerning the key agenda points in hand! At the end of each franchise advisory council meeting, action points and timelines should be documented and allocated to respective team members in order to ensure action and results!

What benefit do they bring?

I think the obvious answer here is: it varies depending on the ongoing effectiveness of the franchise advisory council.

For the franchisor

Having a franchise advisory council means the franchisor can obtain representative feedback without having to regularly take the whole network out of their businesses for meetings. It means decisions and issues can be delivered and discussed in a more personal way, allowing for meaningful dialogue and unity. It creates an opportunity for smoother implementation and buy-in to change with the majority, if not everyone, pulling in the same direction with a clear understanding of the objectives and the bigger picture.

It would be a very blinkered franchisor who assumed that because he or she had built the original business there was nothing left to learn about it. The franchisees are out there every day, dealing with the ups and downs of the business in ever-changing environments, so they will all have a worthwhile story to tell from a unique point of view. Franchisors should be eager to harness this knowledge and an engaged franchise advisory council ought to be an invaluable source.

With the right people on board it should also be a great outlet for creative thinking. There's nothing to say the franchisor or franchisees must select an agenda full of decisions requiring action from, or the approval of, the other. Far from it, franchise advisory council meetings can be a great place to ask questions, encourage debate and unleash creativity. There are plenty of stories of franchisees bringing fantastic ideas and suggestions for improvements and even new product lines.

Of course, in the main, franchise advisory councils are an effective and efficient way for the franchisor to keep the entire network informed and engaged with the progress of the business. Franchisors spend a lot of time and a not inconsiderable amount of money recruiting the best franchisees they can find – they should respect and want their opinions on any matters that could significantly affect the business.

For the franchisee

The very existence of a franchise advisory council should tell you that your franchisor wants to create a harmonious, cohesive network that will strive together to achieve great things for the brand.

Even if you aren't in it, it represents a chance to get closer to the business, to shape decisions, affect change and have a more tangible share in your future.

Support

Starting your own business from scratch can be a very lonely time, and one of the greatest advantages of investing in a franchise is that you have people to talk to when the going gets tough, or to call on when you need help with a decision. Often these people will be fellow franchisees rather than the franchisor. My advice to franchisees is to embrace their franchise advisory council and see it as a vehicle for change, rather than as a platform to get their own way.

Engagement

The franchisor/franchisee relationship is different for every brand. At one end of the scale franchisees are left almost entirely to their own devices and, at the other, some will feel stifled by an overbearing, controlling franchisor. A franchise advisory council should at the very least give every franchisee the option to take a look at what goes on at the central support office and see what changes might be around the corner for the brand they have invested in. Even the most happily independent of franchisee should appreciate the opportunity for better engagement within the bigger picture.

Co-operation

No one likes to have decisions forced upon them. It's actually quite a common reason for people to choose self-employment in the first place. No matter how self-employed you are, there is always someone else who holds at least one trump card over you, whether that be the government, the bank, the taxman or an industry regulator. In franchising it can be all of these things too, but also the franchisors, who will hold you to your franchise agreement that is heavily stacked in their favour (but that forms another chapter of the book!). The franchise advisory council is a wonderful place for co-operation to grow between both parties. The franchisor may well have the ultimate say, but the benefits of having had an open conversation between all concerned parties is surely a good thing in any circumstance?

Suzie McCafferty of Platinum Wave

Case study: Raring2go!

In 2011, I decided to change the front cover design of our Raring2go! magazines. Armed with nothing more than a few ideas and one of my trusted graphic designers, I made some changes and presented the outcome as a 'fait accompli' to my network of franchisees. I sensed a little resistance initially, but in time the network came round and agreed it was a good move and that I had succeeded in developing a refreshing new look.

I was puzzled though. How could I avoid potentially alienating my network in future when I wanted to shake things up? I was determined to ensure future 'change' was embraced from the outset by the entire network. I wasn't sure how I would do this – I just knew it would create a greater harmony within my business and, as a business owner, harmony within the heart of the business is a great ally.

In mid-2012 I spoke with the bfa and listened intently when it recommended that I create a 'franchise council', a representative body of franchisees with whom I could work closely to introduce and effect change at any level within the business. After all, I thought, who better to help me decide on new directions in our business than those people directly affected by such decisions. I instinctively felt this would be a universally welcomed move, and I am pleased to say I was right.

Following guidelines suggested by the bfa I formed our rather pompously named franchisee consultative forum or FCF for short. Our council. We agreed to physically meet twice a year, once in the north and once in the south. Everyone was responsible for their own costs to get there but I would provide lunch and cover the costs of the meeting.

Our first meeting was in late 2013 and I fashioned an agenda by asking the members for their suggestions. Many were presented, which made for an initially very full and perhaps, looking back, a disjointed meeting. By far the most prominent item was a call for a rethink and refresh of our magazine design. In publishing, contemporary and current design is critical, and so we began our work, going into such detail that we consequently also re-wrote our brand guidelines manual at the same time. It really was a beautiful thing to be a part of.

Fast forward to October 2014 and our annual conference, the culmination of more than a year of FCF work – both face to face and via email and telephone calls – and I was about to present the new-look Raring2go! to our expectant audience of franchisees. They all knew the new design had been orchestrated by the FCF and I let them know that in my view the FCF had delivered a stunning new iteration of Raring2go!

While A1-size poster-boards of our new covers were revealed by my colleagues, I saw the franchisees rise to their feet from their seats and begin to applaud. They were applauding the new designs, which they clearly loved, but they were primarily thanking the FCF for being true to the ethos of the network and for delivering a really exciting new look. I knew in that moment that forming the FCF had been by far one of the best decisions I had made in my business. We're working hard now on some other structural changes to our proposition and I know that the FCF involvement in this will ensure we deliver the best possible outcomes for our business, our people and our audiences.

Freddie St George, Franchisor Raring2go!

Focus points

* Not all franchises have franchise councils, but those that do offer you the opportunity to be involved in the development of the network.
* There is no defined structure for a council, so they can be organized in a variety of ways.
* There is also no defined template for governance or topics to be covered.
* Being involved on a council doesn't only provide you with representation, you will also receive support from fellow franchisees.
* Although you may join a council to 'change the world', you will probably find that being involved in the council helps you have a more rounded view of what your franchisor is trying to achieve.

Next step

For those new to franchising, franchise councils are a new area to them. Hopefully, this chapter has helped you see the benefits to both franchisor and franchisee. In the next chapter we will look at the British Franchise Association in more depth.

23

The British Franchise Association

In this chapter you will learn:

- ▶ *What the British Franchise Association is*
- ▶ *What the role of the Association is*
- ▶ *The different levels of membership available.*

This is a guest chapter by Cathryn Hayes of the British Franchise Association.

So, what is the British Franchise Association (bfa) and how did the association come about?

In 1977, eight franchise companies came together to form the British Franchise Association, to represent ethical franchising – based on formal criteria for membership (https://www.thebfa.org/about-bfa/criteria-and-checklist-for-membership) and a code of business practice (https://www.thebfa.org/about-bfa/code-of-ethics). As the UK industry grew and the international stage became more important, the bfa continued to grow both its membership and influence.

Over the years, the bfa has developed into the UK's voluntary self-regulatory body representing ethical franchising. Franchisors and professional advisers to the UK franchise industry wishing to be accredited must put themselves forward to the bfa to be tested against extensive criteria.

Only if they can successfully demonstrate that they meet the standards are they then able to join as a member, gain access to the benefits of membership and be represented by the British Franchise Association.

The franchise industry has grown significantly over the past 30 years and the bfa's role remains to ensure that it retains the highest standards, with a commitment to best practice and robustness – even in the toughest of economic climates.

In the early days, franchising was concentrated in a limited number of markets, predominantly fast food, motor services and hotels – now, there is a wide range of different business sectors represented.

Another change has been the rise of management and investment franchises in addition to the traditional single, 'hands-on' operator and, of course, multi-unit franchisees, where the business can be a multi-million pound operation with thousands of staff. Each business has its own characteristics and pitfalls. Against this changing background, the bfa has updated and developed the core standards and requirements for accreditation, as well as keeping up to date with legal developments that could affect franchising in the UK and beyond. The Standards and Code of Ethics have been reviewed and strengthened over the years to provide guidance to franchisors and their advisers through a series of Technical Bulletins, to expand on and clarify the rules.

In addition to providing information and advice to businesses wanting to franchise or people considering joining a franchise, the bfa also works closely with its members (http://www.thebfa. org/members) to help enhance their expertise in the sector, as well as representing the sector on their behalf in the media and with government and academia.

Another area where the bfa may assist its members is through formal and informal dispute resolution. The bfa can make a positive contribution by supporting the re-establishment of positive communication between the parties, with the aim of bringing about a resolution, without making any judgment.

If this informal approach does not achieve resolution, the bfa has an independent mediation service that is open to both parties to facilitate an amicable resolution. This is a completely voluntary process that involves independent, qualified mediators with recognized expertise in the franchise sector. There is also a more formal arbitration service that can be used, again using an independent and experienced arbitrator.

One of the bfa's roles is running educational seminars for prospective franchisors and franchisees to help them understand how franchising works and the areas to consider. For members, there is a range of specialist seminars and regional forums as well as the annual conference and other events. The bfa focuses strongly on sharing best practice and its experienced, full member franchisors and professional affiliates regularly present at bfa events, to share their good practice with other franchisors and companies who are considering franchising their businesses.

Another important role for the bfa has been promoting the work of the association and its members to enable the sector to showcase what successful franchising looks like. Working with key sponsors, the bfa operates a prestigious and highly sought after Franchisor and Franchisee of the Year Awards programme, as well as publishing a regular industry survey through a respected professional research company.

In addition, the bfa's own website and social media channels are used to provide case studies, advisory articles from members, as well as from the association itself. Key members of the bfa's senior team regularly write articles and present at seminars in wider business publications and organizations too, in order to bring successful, ethical franchising to a wider audience.

The bfa has really been at the forefront of setting the standards and benchmarking what makes a good franchise. The association has also been involved over the years in leading the way in being a standards-based association in Europe and worldwide, through its Board presence on the European Franchise Federation and the World Franchise Council. Most importantly though, all this work is carried out through the support of bfa members, who have committed to comply with the Code of Ethics and rules of behaviour and who support the bfa's work.

QFP

The Qualified Franchise Professional (QFP) has been specially developed for people working within the franchising industry who want to demonstrate their experience, understanding and ethical approach to franchising.

Franchisors, professional advisers to the industry, directors, managers and franchisee support staff are all able to go through the learning programme in order to benefit from the learning and recognition that the QFP provides.

It signifies a highly developed level of expertise and experience in franchising and a thorough understanding of the ethical standards and best practices involved.

As a standards-based franchise qualification built upon the ethics of the bfa, the QFP programme and qualification is open only to principals or employees of bfa member organizations, including affiliated franchising expert advisers.

Unlike membership of the bfa, the QFP is specific to an individual and not to a company. It recognizes the personal commitment, time and continuous professional development of members of the franchising community.

Through attending a number of prequalified events and seminars, individuals gain points towards their QFP – over a period of up to three years. Before achieving the qualification, all candidates must accumulate the appropriate number of points before passing an interview with the QFP Expert Panel.

All events, courses, seminars and forums that make up the core and elective learning for the QFP are provided by the bfa, together with accredited providers Franchise Finance (http://www.franchisefinance.co.uk/) and The Franchise Training Centre (http://thefranchisetrainingcentre.co.uk/).

The Franchise Trust

The Franchise Trust is a registered charity in England and Wales and has been set up to deliver educational courses to develop knowledge, skills and capabilities in business, with priority given to individuals assessed as being in greatest need because of financial hardship, age, ill health and any other reason that may disadvantage those individuals in gaining access to educational opportunities.

The trustees all have a longstanding history in franchising and have demonstrated considerable experience in and commitment to the sector. The bfa's director-general is secretary of the trust, and the association provided the initial funding and support in order to achieve charitable status, but the trust operates independently of the association.

The trust's vision is to ensure that no individual is prevented by circumstances that are not in their power to change (but which the trust can help change) from taking up the opportunities that franchising might otherwise offer them.

Membership of the bfa

FRANCHISOR MEMBERS

At an early stage, the association decided to have a range of membership categories, depending on the stage of development that the particular franchise had reached.

Provisional listing is available at an early stage to businesses with a successful trading record in the UK of at least a year and which are in the process of developing a franchised business. They do not have to have any franchisees at this stage but a pilot operation should be in operation, which could be franchised or company-owned. There will be a franchise agreement that meets the bfa's Code of Ethics and the company has to be able to demonstrate that its development programme is based on good franchising practice. In addition, any projections or estimates of potential income and profitability for franchisees must be based on actual figures that can be proven.

For *Full* and *Associate* membership of the bfa – four key criteria must be met: that the business is viable, transferable, ethical and fully disclosed.

These principles are key to the bfa's accreditation process, which must be passed before membership is granted. As part of their application, franchisors are expected to demonstrate how they meet these standards and provide evidence, where appropriate.

► **Viable:** the franchise will be able to demonstrate that its product or service has a market, i.e. is saleable – at a level of profit that will support a network of franchisees.

► **Transferable:** this means that the 'know-how' underpinning the business can be transferred to and replicated by a different operator at arm's length, which is essential if the business is to be franchised.

► **Ethical:** the franchise must be set up and operated following the ethical principles set out in the European Code of Ethics for Franchising, which covers matters such as recruiting and selection of franchisees, as well as the ongoing support and relationship with them.

▶ **Disclosed:** all material information on the business and franchise, including the legal contract, must be disclosed without any ambiguity or confusion to prospective franchisees.

In addition, Full Members will have a proven trading and franchising record and must demonstrate that they have reached critical mass – where their income from ongoing management services fees more than covers their costs in operating the franchise and their services to franchisees.

Associate Members must fulfil similar requirements to Full Members, but do not need to have as much experience in franchising or as many franchisees. Associate Members are franchisors working their way towards Full Membership.

It all sounds like a lot of hoops to jump through – and it is – but this is vital to ensure that the sector is protected from rogue or inexperienced operators who do not take the right advice. Franchisors who join the bfa know that the standards are key to a thriving and robust industry and will freely share their experience and best practice with newcomers – one of the key benefits of belonging to the bfa 'club'!

FRANCHISEE MEMBERSHIP

In 2010, two franchisees were appointed to the association's board of directors so that the association could start the process of offering membership to franchisees. With the support of its member franchisors, the bfa built a register of franchisees and developed the structure for this new franchisee membership category, with representation and a say in the governance of the bfa in addition to a range of member benefits. A third franchisee was appointed to the board of directors in 2012 and franchisee membership was launched later that year.

A range of benefits has been developed, including discounting training, a legal helpline and an 'everyday savings' portal. Local networking events are being rolled out across the UK and there will be a specific franchisee programme for the first time at the 2016 bfa annual conference.

The continuing work of the three franchisee directors on the bfa board is highly valued by the bfa and demonstrates that franchisees are also concerned with the governance of the association and want to play their part in continuing to help develop the standards and work of the bfa.

PROFESSIONAL ADVISERS – AFFILIATE MEMBERS

The bfa recognized the need to work with the professional advisers (https://www.thebfa.org/members/affiliates) who operate in the franchise sector. This allows potential clients to identify those advisers who have demonstrated that they are working to bfa standards. It also enables the industry to benefit from advice and guidance that these professional advisers provide to help franchisors in developing and enhancing their businesses. Therefore, affiliate membership was created for professional advisers in franchising, who are accredited on the basis of their proven professional skills and the successful application of those skills to franchising. These professional advisers undertake that the advice on franchising that they provide to clients is of a standard consistent with the aims and objectives of the European Code of Ethics.

After a full review of the affiliate membership status, the association decided to limit this membership category to six core discipline areas:

- ▶ Finance (banks and accountants)
- ▶ Legal
- ▶ Franchise consultants (business development)
- ▶ Franchise consultants (recruitment and brokers)
- ▶ Recruitment media – websites
- ▶ Recruitment media – magazines and newspapers.

This was to reflect the fact that these core areas are key to the improvement of standards in franchising and are not only about having a service to sell to franchisors.

The affiliate members have their own regular forums where they meet to discuss the current hot topics in the sector, network and share best practice, and they can also attend the regional forums alongside franchisor members. This is all part of the best practice sharing which the association views as a key part of its role in working to drive up standards across the sector.

SUPPLIERS

As franchising has developed into a substantial community of businesses across a wide variety of industry sectors, the demand for various products and services has also developed.

For those companies who offer services within the franchise sector, but who do not meet the criteria to become an affiliate member, the bfa offers a supplier membership category. This enables the industry to benefit from a range of supplier services and also enables those suppliers who want to be active participants in the sector to have a presence and network with bfa members.

Although these companies do not have to go through the normal detailed accreditation process for bfa members, the association takes references before approving a new supplier. They are then able to exhibit their services at the bfa's annual conference, outline their services to members and, where appropriate, present about their offering at meetings or seminars. A company that fits the affiliate criteria cannot join at the lower accreditation level of a supplier, and any franchisor wishing to offer services as a supplier must first become an accredited bfa member.

Focus points

* The association was formed in 1977 by eight franchisors to represent ethical franchising.
* The association is standards based, and as such membership should provide some level of assurance as to the reputation of the franchisor or the professional adviser.
* There are different levels of franchisor membership based on the size and experience of the franchisor.
* For potential franchisees, the bfa has a wealth of information available on its website, and it provides educational seminars that you can attend.
* Once you have joined a bfa member franchisor, you can join the bfa as a franchisee member at a very low cost to obtain the benefits of membership yourself.

Next step

We've now covered most areas of running a franchise. The next section covers how to exit a franchise, since all good things must come to an end! We'll start with the next chapter, which looks at how a franchise agreement is ended.

Part Eight

Leaving a franchise

Termination of a franchise

In this chapter you will learn:

- ▶ *The ways that a franchise agreement can be ended*
- ▶ *What will be required of you once the agreement ends*
- ▶ *Why a franchisor might decide to terminate your agreement early.*

They say that 'all good things come to an end', and at some point you will find that the franchise relationship has come to an end. Broadly speaking, this will happen for a number of reasons:

► The franchise agreement has expired

► The franchisee wants to leave the network (perhaps the network wasn't as promised initially)

► The franchisor wants to 'exit' the franchisee (perhaps the franchisee isn't adhering to the agreement)

► The franchisee wants to sell the business as a going concern (covered in the next chapter).

I have asked some of my legal colleagues to provide you with some expert advice around the first three points (see below), together with some practical advice from a franchisor.

Remember this: Advice from a franchisor

It is important to remember that **if you risk damaging the franchisor's precious brand, they only have one option**. They can't fine you, throw things at you or lock you up (unless their franchise agreement says so, which is highly unlikely) so all they can do is remove the franchise from you. This won't be done lightly, but **they have a duty to all other franchisees (from which you will also benefit) to protect the brand at all costs**, so if a franchisee is endangering that, then he or she will have to leave. This may mean you are left with a lease on a building that you can't use, a large outstanding bank loan that you will still need to repay, potentially some staff liabilities, and possibly even a claim from the franchisor for his loss of income. You really don't want to put your franchisor in a position where he or she has no option but to act decisively; but the good news is, it can be really easily avoided. Follow the system at all times, and if you feel like straying from it, just remember to ask first and you'll be fine.

Steve Felmingham, Banana Moon Day Nurseries

Key idea: Advice from an expert

The usual ways in which a franchise relationship will come to an amicable end are:

✳ on the expiry of the franchise agreement
✳ on the sale of the franchisee's business as a going concern to either the franchisor or a new, approved franchisee
✳ (less common) on mutually agreed early termination of the franchise agreement.

Whatever the reason, the following issues need to be considered.

The franchisee will be required to cease all use of the brand and the system from the effective date of termination. In some ways, operating a franchise is similar to renting a flat: during the term of tenancy, you benefit from the exclusive use and full enjoyment of the flat, but when the tenancy expires you hand back the keys to the landlord, leave and you have no further rights to occupy or enjoy the flat. Equally, on expiry of a franchise, the franchisee has to hand back all of the tangible and intangible aspects of its business which are connected to the franchise system and the associated trademarks.

The franchisee will be bound by certain post-termination restrictions, which may include non-disclosure of confidential information (which might last indefinitely) and undertaking not to operate a competing business or contact suppliers, customers or solicit staff (which will usually last between 6 and 12 months).

Non-competition and non-solicitation undertakings usually have a geographical scope and are designed to prevent a franchisee from operating a competing business from the same premises at which it operated the franchise business, or within a certain radius of those premises, or within a wider territory, particularly in areas where the franchisor or its other franchisees operate.

From a legal perspective, these types of restrictions are enforceable provided they are proportionate to protecting the franchisor's legitimate business interests and know-how. On leaving a franchise network, a franchisee can become a competitor overnight, so the law recognizes that a franchisor has a genuine interest in trying to preserve the franchisee's former patch and appoint a new franchisee in his or her place. However, these restrictions should not stray into becoming 'restraint of trade' clauses, which effectively prevent a franchisee from earning a living after the end of the franchise.

The franchise agreement will usually give the franchisor the right to step in and operate the franchisee's business (which can become complicated in premises-based franchises where third-party landlords are involved) **and buy back the franchisee's assets.** The purchase price of an asset buy-back will be on the basis of the net realizable value of the physical assets in the business (stock, equipment, fixtures & fittings, etc) but with no attribution of goodwill or going-concern value, on the basis that the franchise agreement has ended and the post-termination restrictions kick in (so there is no going-concern value) and the goodwill is associated with the trademarks, and is therefore the property of the franchisor.

This situation differs if the franchisee is exercising a right to sell the business during the term of the franchise agreement. Again, the post-termination restrictions will still apply to the outgoing franchisee, but it will be able to realize the going concern value of the value, which is usually calculated as multiple of annual profit.

The key takeaway for franchisees who are preparing to exit their franchise is to first understand what the franchise agreement says about post-termination and formulate a plan for what the franchisee will do during such time as the post-termination restrictions apply. If neither the franchisor nor an incoming franchisee purchases the assets on the franchisee's business, it could be left with equipment, staff and a lease and it will need to either redeploy or dispose of those assets in a way that does not put it in breach of the franchise agreement.

Gordon Drakes, Field Fisher

Key idea: Advice from an expert

Although a franchise agreement will last for a fixed term, often five years, subject to a right to renew, there are circumstances when it can be brought to an end earlier.

Typically, the agreement will provide the franchisor with a contractual right to terminate in certain defined circumstances, usually in the context of breach of contract by the franchisee.

Termination by the franchisor can be effected immediately, without a warning, in circumstances of serious breach, such as ceasing to trade or threatening to do so, insolvency, trading through a competing business, misuse of the brand, etc. It could also be effected if the franchisor issues a warning which the franchisee ignores, such as a failure to pay fees on time, deliver reports of turnover or accounts. If the franchisee is in repeated breach over the course of a year the franchisor could terminate immediately. This is often described as a 'three strikes and you're out' rule although some agreements will provide for it to apply after just two breaches in a year.

If the franchisor terminates the agreement then the franchisee has to immediately cease trading under the brand, using the intellectual property and the system. The franchisee is also likely to be required to cease trading in any similar or competing business in the territory for up to 12 months and to not solicit work from any current or former customers. They can be required to transfer premises, hand over customer data, telephone numbers and to sell to the franchisor stock and equipment. These contractual terms are designed to allow the franchisor to retain the goodwill in the brand in the territory and either continue trading there itself or look to recruit a replacement franchisee to take over the territory.

Sometimes franchisors get it wrong and they terminate when they do not have the legal right to do so. This amounts to a repudiatory breach of contract by the franchisor, which the franchisee can accept and try to continue trading without restriction or claim compensation. It can be difficult to get a court order requiring the franchisor to permit the franchisee to continue trading under the brand. The mutual trust and confidence required between a franchisor and franchisee would have broken down. It would be very hard to continue to operate within the brand and the network in those circumstances and usually the franchisee's remedy would be to claim compensation.

Very rarely will a franchisee have a contractual right to bring the contract to an end before the expiry of the term. Some agreements, such as those in relation to education tuition, may contain a contractual right to give notice without reason, at any time. Most will only reserve the right to the franchisor to terminate for reasons of franchisee breach. However, that does not mean a franchisee is powerless when they are confronted by some material failure on the part of the franchisor. A franchisee will have a right to terminate an agreement in certain circumstances if the franchisor has committed a fundamental or repudiatory breach of contract. This must go to the heart of the agreement. Examples would be a failure to hand over money collected by the franchisor but due to the franchisee. Other issues may arise over the franchisee's sense of exclusivity in its territory and the ownership of customers. Increasing use of websites by franchisors to generate sales can appear to cut across a franchisee's right to market the business in their territory and this can cause tension. In some circumstances the franchisor can be in breach of contract, although this very much depends upon the particular contractual terms about the nature of any exclusivity and reserved rights in relation to the Internet or national customers.

Franchisees may also have the right to bring the agreement to an early end if they discover that the franchisor has misrepresented the opportunity to them. This is a complex area but recent examples include franchisors misrepresenting the likely financial performance of a new franchise or the number of failures/terminations they have had in recent years. If a franchisee can demonstrate that representations were made falsely, which they relied upon, and they act promptly they can rescind or 'undo' the agreement and/or claim compensation.

Russell Ford, director Owen White Solicitors

Key idea: Advice from an expert

Restrictive covenants typically impose restrictions on a franchisee from competing with the franchisor and/or soliciting or poaching the franchisor's clients, suppliers, employees and other franchisees. From a legal perspective such provisions are typically caught by competition law principles.

In terms of enforcement, **if a franchisee is in breach of in-term non-compete or restrictive covenants, the franchisor's initial course of action may be to terminate the franchise agreement.** Following termination, the franchisor will either bring a claim against the franchisee for breach of contract or, depending on the nature of the franchisee's breach, apply for an injunction to compel the franchisee to either cease their infringing conduct or to comply with their obligations, if appropriate. If the franchisor is successful in a contractual claim, the likely remedies include damages to compensate the franchisor for any losses it has suffered and potentially an account of profits that the franchisee has made from the competing business.

In the case of Carewatch Care Services Limited *v.* Focus Caring Services Limited and others, the High Court held and reaffirmed the position that restrictive covenants may be enforceable if it can be proven that they were designed to protect the company's legitimate business interests and went no further than necessary to achieve that purpose.

Under competition law principles, post-termination non-compete provisions are prohibited unless the franchisor's know-how is dependent on such provisions. In accordance with the EU Vertical Block Exemption (VBE), which provides an exemption to certain competition law principles, such know-how is required to be 'secret', which is a difficult threshold for most franchisors to prove. If such know-how is deemed secret then the VBE recognizes the right for franchisors to impose 12-month non-compete restrictions from the premises at which the franchisee operated its business.

Fortunately, English case law has taken a more sensible approach than that set out in the VBE, recognizing that a wider post-termination geographical restriction may be permitted provided the aim of such provision is to prevent the franchisor's know-how being used by competitors.

Enforcement of post-termination restrictive covenants will typically involve the franchisor applying to the court for an order injuncting the former franchisee (i.e. preventing it from trading or otherwise acting in breach of its covenants).

Post-termination restrictive covenants will only be upheld if the court considers them reasonable. Typically, the court will look at the geographical width of the restriction and the duration. A 12-month restriction not to operate a competing business in the franchisee's former territory is likely to be enforceable whereas a 24-month restriction for the whole of the United Kingdom is likely to constitute an unlawful restraint of the former franchisee's right to trade. Each case will, however, be examined on its own facts.

The franchisor does have discretion as to whether to waive the enforcement of either in-term and/or post-term restrictive covenants but doing so can be commercially dangerous and potentially very damaging for the franchisor's brand.

Graeme Payne, partner Bird & Bird

Focus points

✳ There are a few reasons why a franchise agreement might end.

✳ If you are parting ways amicably, you need to remember that there will likely still be some obligations on you after the agreement has ended.

✳ A franchisor has an obligation to the rest of the network to end the agreement of any franchisee that is damaging the brand.

✳ Sometimes, a franchisee has a legal right to terminate the agreement, if there is a material breach of contract, or if the opportunity had been misrepresented to them.

✳ If in doubt, take legal advice!

Next step

In this chapter we've covered what are possibly the worst-case scenarios for a franchisee – the expiry, or early termination of a franchise agreement. For most franchisees, the end goal is a successful resale of their business, and our final chapter covers just that.

Franchise resales

In this chapter you will learn:

- ► *How a franchise resale works*
- ► *How a franchise is valued*
- ► *What can help increase that value.*

As mentioned in the last chapter, the ideal end goal for most franchisees is a successful resale of their franchise. There is an active market of franchises for sale, and many investors look to purchase successful franchises so that they can have a profitable business from day one.

How does a franchise resale work?

In general, a franchise resale works in a very similar way to any other business sale. The business is put on the market, at a valuation decided by the seller. There is almost always a negotiation on the price and the terms of the sale, and at this point solicitors are appointed on both sides. Together with the bankers, all parties will look towards concluding the deal... The observant reader might have noticed a missing part in the above paragraph though!

With a franchise resale, the franchisor will be keen to ensure that the incoming buyer is suitable for the network. Much in the same way that they spent time and effort in recruiting the right franchisee to build the business, they will want to ensure that their brand is represented in the right way going forwards.

Most franchisors also include a clause within their agreement that permits them to charge a fee on successful resale, which may vary depending on whether the franchisor sources the purchaser on your behalf.

Key idea: Advice from an expert

Franchisors tend to concentrate on new franchisees buying new sites and certainly in the early days of franchising they don't really pay much attention to the idea of resales in their group. So when a franchisee decides to sell or leave the group the process can become a bit hit and miss.

As more resales happen the franchisor will become better equipped to deal with them and understand that getting new blood into what can sometimes have become a static environment is a great way to grow the business. Then they really do start to look seriously at their processes. Even so, it can prove to be a really time consuming process so it's a good idea to have either a dedicated staff member or to outsource the process.

The process is quite different to a new start in that the purchaser is looking at a going concern often with staff and equipment in place from day one. So before they begin to think about the franchise they often want to explore the accounts and the business first. This is okay, but they need to remember that they are buying a franchise and the franchisor should be having a meeting at an early stage to establish whether they are suitable to join the group – or not as the case may be. Letting them meet with the selling franchisee first can be a mistake, as the franchisee gets excited with the idea of having a purchaser and can be very disappointed when the franchisor says no.

Once a suitable buyer is found most franchisors will expect to see a business plan and a profit & loss account. This will be prepared by the buyer who will be working on this as the terms of the sale are being agreed.

The discussions around this might include negotiations over the price of the business, and negotiations with the landlord of any premises involved. All of this needs to be agreed before the Sale and Purchase Agreement (SPA) can be produced by the franchisor's solicitors.

There will normally be three solicitors involved in the sale and purchase. The franchisor's solicitor and the buyer and seller will each instruct their own solicitors. It's normal for the franchisor's solicitor's fees to be shared by the buyer and the seller.

Fees for selling can vary depending on the scale of the business and solicitors will quote to each party accordingly. The franchisor will have fees due to them from both the buyer and the seller and these are normally outlined in the franchise agreement and need to be accounted for in the budgeting of the franchisee selling and the buyer's profit & loss account presented to the bank and to the franchisor.

Exchange will normally take place prior to training and completion after training, with all fees due to the franchisor as part of the purchase being paid by the purchaser at the time of exchange.

The important thing with resales is finding the correct buyer, because once a franchise gets to resale stage it's usually a management franchise, so franchisors need to be really careful who they are passing the baton to, and someone who is suitable as a cold start franchisee is not always the best person for a resale. Best advice is get advice when you start your franchising journey so that you are prepared for the inevitable.

Julie Taylor, Managing Director Franchise Resales

How is a franchise valued?

One of the main advantages of being in a franchise is that there are several other businesses similar to yours, so a track record of business valuations has already been determined. There is a saying that business valuation is an art rather than a science, as there are so many variables involved, including:

▶ Economic conditions

▶ Stability of business

▶ Systemization of business

▶ Dependence on large customers

▶ Dependence on owner

▶ Level of discretionary expenses included in business

▶ Reason for sale

▶ Urgency of sale

▶ Negotiation process

▶ Structure of sale (asset sale or share sale).

Having said all of that, being in a franchise enables you to at least have a benchmark based on previous franchise resales.

Broadly speaking, there are two different ways of valuing a business – either by valuing the assets of the business (break-up value) or the value of the future profits. The break-up value is only used for businesses that have no underlying value in their trade, so often the valuation of the likely future profits is used. To calculate this, a valuer would ordinarily look at historic profits, adjust them for any items that need 'reconstituting' (i.e. extraordinary expenses incurred), and then apply a 'price/earnings' multiplier to the figure to determine the valuation based on profitability. This will be added to the market value of any assets held to derive the end valuation of the business.

As mentioned in the list above, the structure of the sale can impact on the valuation of the business. This is an area that you will need professional advice on in respect of your own personal circumstances, from both an accountant and a legal adviser.

Key idea: Advice from an expert

If your franchise is mainly operated by national accounts/contracts from the franchisor and doesn't have very many local contracts/customers then the business is in a very dangerous position. If the franchisor lost the account/contract with the national supplier what would happen to your business? In some instances I've seen that they have to close. Now is this the fault of the franchisor or franchisee? It comes down to both: the franchisor shouldn't be letting the franchisee only operate on national contracts but on the other hand the franchisee shouldn't be relying on them either. The stronger the local contacts in your area/franchise the more saleable the franchise is.

All business owners go through what is called the **curve of emotion**. When you start your business/franchise you are happy and excited about being a business owner, going to meetings, clinching deals and making money, then you start to get complacent and relying on your current customers and the business starts to drop a little. You may have taken on staff and spent a lot of time and money on training them up, then they find their feet and you get a new lease of life and the business starts to go on to the next level. Then you start to rely on your staff but still doing the sales because you know what happened last time cannot happen again, so you spend more time with the family or on the golf course and the business is ticking by, then a competitor starts in your area and some of your customers start leaving and you then have to work harder to keep it going, and on and on it goes. During this time you pay your accountancy fees for them to save you money, this then reduces your bottom line but saves your tax bill, personal or corporation tax.

When do you think that most people think about selling their business? When they are doing well and the business is making money or when it becomes hard work and they are thinking of doing something different? Exactly! When the business is not fulfilling their needs anymore. Most of the time this is when I get the 'I want to sell my business' call. I say most of the time; some franchisees do have an exit plan and they do work to it. These are the ones who are going to achieve a high sale value.

When you started your business you would have had a business plan. It's the A4 fancy booklet you put together for the franchisor or lenders. You may or may not have included in your business plan your exit strategy. If you didn't you need to do one now. How do you know where you want to go if you haven't set a destination? What do I mean by an exit strategy? I mean what are you going to do with your business? Are you going to close it, pass it on to your children, or are you going to sell it?

How much do you want for your business? Some of you will have no idea; others will have a figure in mind. If you are thinking that you want to achieve £500k for your business then you have to make the business worth £500k, a business is valued on historical figures normally. Independent accountants use a multiple of Sustainable Transferable Operating Profit (STOP) to establish the value of a business, then averaged over three years weighted towards the latest results. This is the 'norm'. However, different sectors value differently.

You have instructed an accountant to do what accountants do: reduce profit – legally of course. However, hiding all of your money in lots of genuine, different ways will affect your franchise's valuation. This is why franchisors usually take their MSF (management service fee) from the turnover, because if they didn't then you wouldn't make any.

It can take two-to-three years to create the perfect business model for sale. You have to start putting everything through the business and make the profit line more attractive. You also have to make sure the business is still growing: declining trends and flatlining trends will make your business less attractive to an incoming buyer. I'm not saying you won't sell the business, just that you won't receive what you want to achieve for the business.

Michael Bohan, Franchise Resales

Focus points

* A franchise resale typically works in the same way as a general business sale; however, the franchisor will have some involvement.
* The franchisor will take a keen interest about who the new franchisee is; you cannot just sell the business to anyone!
* Often, a franchise resale will only be possible once the franchise has been developed to a 'management' franchise – it's very difficult to sell a job.
* They say that business valuation is an art, not a science. Luckily, in franchising you will usually find that other franchisees provide you with a track record of successful resales, helping you work out a rough valuation of your business.

Conclusion

I hope that you have found this book useful in some way! As mentioned throughout, from both the text and the contributions, franchising is a fantastic opportunity for you to achieve your dream of business ownership, provided that you enter into it with your eyes open and perform your due diligence.

I'd like to take this opportunity to wish you the best of luck in your new venture, and please let me know how you get on:

Twitter – www.twitter.com/CarlReader

Facebook – www.facebook.com/CarlReader

Website – www.carlreader.com

Appendix 1: Top Ten Tips

Top ten tips for choosing, starting and running a franchise

1   Start with the end in mind, and work out your desired exit strategy

2   Make sure you know how much you can afford

3   Make sure that it is a business that you are excited and passionate about

4   Remember that the success of the franchise comes down to you

5   Take professional advice from franchise experts along the way

6   Don't be afraid to ask the right questions

7   Do your due diligence

8   Make sure you are comfortable with who you will be dealing with at head office, and the culture of the business

9   Make sure your family are comfortable with your choice as this is a life changing decision

10 Enjoy the whole process!

Appendix 2: Sample Franchise Agreement

The sample franchise agreement has been provided by Jane Masih, Director, Owen White Solicitors.

****

DATED _____ 201[ ]

[*Name of Franchisor*] **LIMITED (1)**

and

[*Name of Franchisee*] **(2)**

FRANCHISE AGREEMENT

(SOLE TRADER/PARTNERSHIP)

THIS AGREEMENT is made the   day of   201[ ]

BETWEEN

1. 'Franchisor'   [   ] **LIMITED** incorporated in England (No) whose registered office is at [   ]

2. 'Franchisee'   [   ] of [   ]

BACKGROUND

A. The Franchisor has expended considerable effort money skill and time and has acquired experience and expertise establishing and developing the [   ] **Service**

B. The Franchisor offers to the Franchisee a valuable system of technical information and management advice assistance and support in the operation of the [   ] **Service** and in methods of and benefiting from marketing advertising research and promotion of the [   ] **Service**

C. The Franchisor has established a reputation demand and goodwill for the [   ] **Service** and has established a reputation in the United Kingdom for the Intellectual Property (including the Franchisor's name and logo) Knowhow livery and other identifying materials signifying the highest standards of design quality marketing skill and service

D. The Franchisee wishes to acquire from the Franchisor a franchise to offer and supply the [   ] **Service**

NOW IT IS AGREED AS FOLLOWS

1. DEFINITIONS

In this Agreement the following expressions have the meanings set out opposite to them:-

'Accounts and Records'	complete and accurate books of account records of transactions and other internal records of the Business which the Franchisee shall keep in accordance with the provisions of this Agreement and the Manual as amended by the Franchisor from time to time in its absolute discretion
'Business'	the Franchisee's business of the offer and provision of the [ ] **Service**
'Commencement Date'	the commencement date of this Agreement as set out in Schedule 2
'Equipment'	the equipment to be used by the Franchisee in the Business as more particularly set out in Schedule 3 as amended by the Franchisor from time to time in its absolute discretion
'Expiry Date'	the expiry date of this Agreement as set out in Schedule 2
'Gross Sales'	the sum total of all sales receipts and receivables (whether or not payment is made) of the Business calculated on an accrual basis excluding value added tax paid to HM Revenue and Customs including (without limitation) any uncollected credit accounts and any estimated or any assumed gross revenues received by or offered to the Franchisee arising out of any business interruption insurance claims
'Initial Fee'	the initial franchise fee to be paid by the Franchisee to the Franchisor in the amount and in accordance with the terms more particularly set out in Schedule 2 and in this Agreement

'Intellectual Property'	the Knowhow trade name(s) trade mark(s) design right(s) copyright logo(s) design(s) symbol(s) insignia including but not limited to the intellectual property described or referred to in Schedule 4 or otherwise in this Agreement as amended by the Franchisor from time to time in its absolute discretion
'Knowhow'	the package of non-patented practical information resulting from experience and testing by the Franchisor which is substantial and identified in the Manual
'Management Services Fee'	the management services fee payable by the Franchisee to the Franchisor in the amount and in the manner set out in this Agreement in consideration for the continuing advice and support to be provided by the Franchisor as set out in this Agreement
'Manual'	the operating training and any other manual setting out the written part of the System to be used by the Franchisee in the Business as amended by the Franchisor from time to time in its absolute discretion
'Minimum Performance Criteria'	the minimum sales targets and the minimum local marketing spend commitment to be achieved by the Franchisee throughout the Term as more particularly set out in this Agreement and Schedule 6
'Month'	a calendar month

'Nominated Suppliers'	the suppliers selected by the Franchisor from which the Franchisee shall exclusively purchase Equipment as listed in the Manual and as amended by the Franchisor from time to time in its absolute discretion
'Premises'	the premises listed in Schedule 2 or any alternative premises as may be expressly approved in writing by the Franchisor
'Stationery'	report forms order forms quotations invoices notepaper letter headings compliment slips business cards and other stationery consumed in the Business as set out in the Manual and as amended by the Franchisor from time to time in its absolute discretion
'Substantial Term'	a term of this Agreement set out in Schedule 5 a breach of which entitles the Franchisor to terminate this Agreement with immediate effect
'System'	the systems methods techniques operating procedures programmes programs processes trade secrets confidential information Knowhow marketing advertising research and promotional techniques including without limitation those set out in the Manual using the Intellectual Property which have been developed and adopted by the Franchisor for use in the operation of businesses offering and providing the [ ] **Service** as amended by the Franchisor from time to time in its absolute discretion
'Term'	the period set out in Schedule 2

'Territory'	the geographical area which for the purpose of identification only is highlighted on the map set out in Schedule 1
'Vehicle'	a vehicle approved by the Franchisor to be signed as directed by the Franchisor and used by the Franchisee in the operation of the Business
'Website'	the website www.[owned by and/or operated on behalf of the Franchisor
'[ ] Service'	the offer and provision of [ ] using the System and the Intellectual Property

2. GRANT OF FRANCHISE

2.1 The Franchisor grants to the Franchisee a franchise subject to and in accordance with the terms and conditions of this Agreement:-

    2.1.1 to offer and supply the [   ] **Service**

    2.1.2 in the Territory

    2.1.3 using the System and the Intellectual Property

    [*insert other relevant conditions*]

3. COMMENCEMENT OF FRANCHISE AND TERM

This Agreement shall commence on the Commencement Date and shall continue in force for the Term and shall expire on the Expiry Date unless terminated earlier in accordance with this Agreement

4. OPTION TO RENEW

4.1 At the end of the Term the Franchisee will have the right to enter into a new franchise agreement with the Franchisor **PROVIDED THAT ALL** of the following conditions are fulfilled:

[*insert other relevant conditions*]

5. FEES AND OTHER PAYMENTS

5.1 The Franchisee shall pay to the Franchisor during the continuance of this Agreement without formal notice or demand and without abatement set-off or deduction:

5.1.1 the Initial Fee which shall be payable in full on signing this Agreement

5.1.2 the Management Services Fee which shall be equal to ten per cent of Gross Sales The Management Services Fee shall be paid on the tenth day of each Month in respect of Gross Sales of the immediately preceding Month

[*insert other relevant payment provisions*]

6. ACCOUNTS AND RECORDS

6.1 The Franchisee must maintain Accounts and Records in accordance with the procedure in the Manual which are sufficient to show and explain the transactions of the Business and shall be such as to disclose accurately the financial position of the Business at any time

[*insert other relevant conditions*]

7. THE PREMISES

7.1 The Franchisee at his expense shall:

[*insert relevant conditions*]

8. THE FRANCHISOR'S OBLIGATIONS

8.1 Initial Obligations

The Franchisor will assist the Franchisee in the commencement of the Business by:

[*insert other relevant conditions*]

8.2 Continuing Obligations

The Franchisor will during the continuance of this Agreement:-

[*insert other relevant conditions*]

9. INTELLECTUAL PROPERTY AND SYSTEM

9.1 The Franchisor warrants that it is entitled to use and license others to use the Intellectual Property throughout the term of this Agreement The Franchisee agrees that he will not in any way infringe or harm the rights of the Franchisor or of any other person to the Intellectual Property

[*insert other relevant conditions*]

10. EQUIPMENT

In order to ensure uniformity and control of high standards in the [   ] **Service** the Franchisee shall purchase Equipment exclusively from Nominated Suppliers or other franchisees of the Franchisor.

[*insert other relevant conditions*]

11. TRAINING

11.1 The Franchisor shall provide an initial training programme for the Franchisee as more particularly described in the Manual

[*insert relevant other conditions*]

12. CONTROL OF STANDARDS AND MANUAL

12.1 The Franchisor and Franchisee mutually accept and agree the necessity in the public interest of achieving and maintaining the highest standards of quality skill and service in the provision of the [   ] **Service** and that all the provisions of this Agreement the Schedules and Manual are necessary in pursuit of these agreed objectives

[*insert other relevant conditions*]

13. CONFIDENTIALITY

[*insert relevant conditions*]

14. FRANCHISEE'S OBLIGATIONS

The Franchisee at his expense during the continuance of this Agreement shall:-

[*insert relevant conditions*]

15. RESTRICTIONS ON FRANCHISEE

15.1 During the continuance of this Agreement the Franchisee shall NOT:

[*insert relevant conditions*]

16. MARKETING ADVERTISING RESEARCH AND PROMOTIONS

16.1 The Franchisor shall maintain administer and promote local regional and national advertising by such marketing advertising research and promotion as may be decided upon from time to time by the Franchisor in its absolute discretion

16.2 The Franchisee shall at his own expense market advertise research and promote the [   ] **Service** within the Territory on a day to day basis as more particularly set out in the Manual The Franchisee shall spend not less than the Minimum Local Marketing Spend each year of the Term and shall obtain the Franchisor's prior written approval for any advertisement or marketing research or promotional material concept or programme which shall differ in any way from the marketing advertising or promotional materials concepts or programmes set out in the Manual or otherwise specified by the Franchisor from time to time

[*insert other relevant conditions*]

17. VEHICLE

The Franchisee at his expense shall:

[*Insert other relevant conditions*]

18. INSURANCE

18.1 The Franchisee shall during the continuance of this Agreement:-

[*insert other relevant conditions*]

19. INDEMNITY

[*insert other relevant conditions*]

20. IMPROVEMENTS

[*insert other relevant conditions*]

21. FORCE MAJEURE

22. SALE OF BUSINESS

22.1 The Franchisor shall be entitled to sell or assign the benefit and the burden of this Agreement at any time

22.2 The Franchisee shall not be entitled to assign this Agreement but shall be entitled to sell the whole of the Business, but not part of the Business, subject to the terms set out in this clause 22 and **PROVIDED THAT**:-

[*insert relevant conditions*]

23. INCAPACITY OR DEATH OF FRANCHISEE

23.1 If the Franchisee or any one of them shall die or become permanently incapacitated the surviving Franchisee (if any) or the personal representatives or receiver (whichever is appropriate) of the deceased or permanently incapacitated Franchisee shall inform the Franchisor in writing of the event within twenty eight days of its occurrence.

[*insert additional relevant conditions*]

24. TERMINATION

24.1 The Franchisor shall have the right to terminate this Agreement with immediate effect by notice in writing to the Franchisee in any of the following circumstances:-

[*insert relevant conditions*]

25. CONDITIONS FOLLOWING TERMINATION

Immediately upon expiry or the termination for any reason
of this Agreement or on the sale of the Business or upon the
Franchisee ceasing to carry on the Business the Franchisee shall:

[*insert relevant conditions*]

26. NOTICES

[*insert relevant conditions*]

27. RESERVATION OF RIGHTS

All rights not expressly and specifically granted to the
Franchisee by this Agreement are reserved to the Franchisor

28. ARBITRATION

[*insert relevant conditions*]

29. INTERPRETATION

30. [*in each case insert relevant conditions*]

30.1 Cumulative Remedies and Waiver

30.2 All clauses severable

30.3 Restrictions reasonable

30.4 Survival of Obligations

30.5 Entire Agreement

30.6 No representations

30.7 No Agency

30.8 No oral representations by agents

30.9 Gender Number and Joint and Several Obligations

30.10 Headings and Statutory References

30.11 Proper Law and Jurisdiction

30.12 Third Party Rights

SCHEDULE 1

Territory

SCHEDULE 2

Particulars

Commencement Date:	day of	20
Expiry Date:	day of	20
Term:	Six years from the Commencement Date	

Premises:

Initial Franchise Fee

SCHEDULE 3

Equipment and Nominated Suppliers

SCHEDULE 4

Intellectual Property

SCHEDULE 5

Substantial Terms

SCHEDULE 6

Minimum Gross Sales Criteria

Signed by [   ]
For and on behalf of [Franchisor] Limited
In the presence of:
Witness name, address and occupation

Signed by [insert name of Franchisee]
In the presence of:
Witness name, address and occupation

Index